EXMOOR
NATIONAL PARK

EXMOOR
NATIONAL PARK

Glyn Court

MICHAEL JOSEPH

Acknowledgements
I wish to thank most warmly Dr Leonard Curtis and
Brian Pearce of the Exmoor National Park for their willing
and expert help and advice at all times, and my wife for
her unfailing patience and support.

The photographs for this book were taken by Brian
Pearce.

First published in Great Britain 1987 by
Webb & Bower (Publishers) Limited
9 Colleton Crescent, Exeter, Devon EX2 4BY
in association with Michael Joseph Limited
27 Wright's Lane, London W8 5SL
and The Countryside Commission,
John Dower House, Crescent Place,
Cheltenham, Glos GL50 3RA

Designed by Ron Pickless

Production by Nick Facer/Rob Kendrew

Illustrations by Rosamund Gendle/Ralph Stobart

Text and new photographs Copyright © The Countryside Commission
Illustrations Copyright © Webb & Bower (Publishers) Ltd

British Library Cataloguing in Publication Data
The National parks of Britain.
Exmoor
1. National parks and reserves — England —
Guide-books 2. England — Description and
travel — 1971- — Guide-books.
I. Court, Glyn
914.2'04858 SB484.G7.

ISBN 0–86350–141–9

Typeset in Great Britain by Keyspools Ltd., Golborne, Lancs.

Printed and bound in Hong Kong by Mandarin Offset.

Contents

	Preface	6
	Introduction	7
1	The making of Exmoor	11
2	Early man on the Moor	22
3	The Forest	29
4	The village	37
5	The Knights of Exmoor	44
6	The Moor after the Knights	52
7	Buildings of Exmoor	60
8	Exmoor at work	70
9	Legend and tradition	80
10	Exmoor wildlife	90
11	Farming on the Moor	105
12	The national park today	111
	Selected places of interest	119
	Glossary	123
	Bibliography	124
	Useful addresses	125
	Index	126

Preface

Exmoor is one of ten national parks which were established in the 1950s. These largely upland and coastal areas represent the finest landscapes in England and Wales and present us all with opportunities to savour breathtaking scenery, to take part in invigorating outdoor activities, to experience rural community life, and most importantly, to relax in peaceful surroundings.

The designation of national parks is the product of those who had the vision, more than fifty years ago, to see that ways were found to ensure that the best of our countryside should be recognized and protected, that the way of life therein should be sustained, and that public access for open-air recreation should be encouraged.

As the government planned Britain's post-war reconstruction, John Dower, architect, rambler and national park enthusiast, was asked to report on how the national park ideal adopted in other countries could work for England and Wales. An important consideration was the ownership of land within the parks. Unlike other countries where large tracts of land are in public ownership, and thus national parks can be owned by the nation, here in Britain most of the land within the national parks was, and still is, privately owned. John Dower's report was published in 1945 and its recommendations accepted. Two years later another report drafted by a committee chaired by Sir Arthur Hobhouse proposed an administrative system for the parks, and this was embodied in the National Parks and Access to the Countryside Act 1949.

This Act set up the National Parks Commission to designate national parks and advise on their administration. In 1968 the National Parks Commission became the Countryside Commission but we continue to have national responsibility for our national parks which are administered by local government, either through committees of the county councils or independent planning boards.

This guide to the landscape, settlements and natural history of Exmoor National Park is one of a series on all ten parks. As well as helping the visitor appreciate the park and its attractions, the guides outline the achievements of and pressures facing the national park authorities today.

Our national parks are a vital asset, and we all have a duty to care for and conserve them. Learning about the parks and their value to us all is a crucial step in creating more awareness of the importance of the national parks so that each of us can play our part in seeing that they are protected for all to enjoy.

Sir Derek Barber
Chairman
Countryside Commission

Introduction

To stand for the first time on Dunkery Beacon, the highest point on Exmoor, on a crystal clear morning in early summer when the rain is over and gone and the singing of birds is heard in the land, and to gaze on the panorama that surrounds you, is to enjoy an unforgettable experience of harmony and variety in the natural and man-made landscape. Your eye can traverse the unhindered distant view from west to east and circuit the southern horizon, and at every moment find some new object of admiration, some region whose people have woven the complex web of creation, rivalries and friendships that make up our national history.

To the north west lies the national park of the Pembrokeshire coast with its heritage of natural beauty and racial characteristics of Wales, England, Norway, Normandy and Flanders; to the north, Gower, with the distant Cambrian Mountains, Brecon Beacons and Black Mountains beyond. The gaze moves on to the Forest of Dean and perhaps the Malvern Hills, and then eastward to the dim silver thread of the River Severn, the Vale of Gloucester and the southern bastions of the Cotswolds. Following round, you see nearer at hand the North Somerset plain, the Mendips, the well-farmed Blackdown Hills on the Devon border, with

Morning mist over the Exe below Milton, Exton.

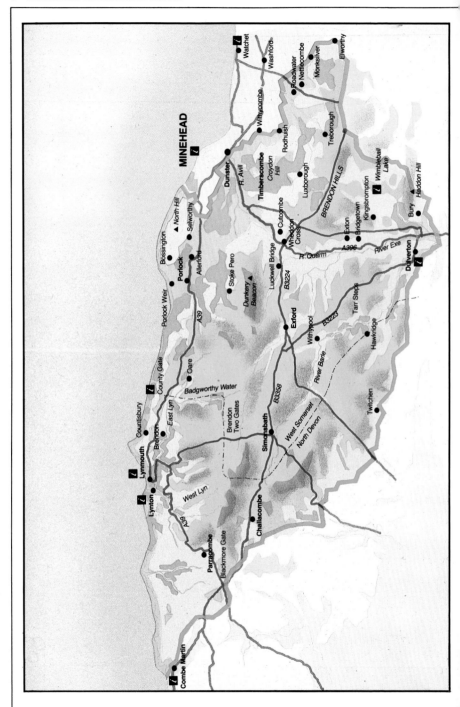

Facing Exmoor National Park.

Sidmouth Gap and, if really clear, a sparkle of the English Channel beyond. Southward, across the uplands of mid-Devon, the tors of Dartmoor rise in clear, serrated outline, and beyond them again, to the south west, the heartland of east Cornwall, Brown Willy and Rough Tor on Bodmin Moor. Now the circuit is nearly complete – south west and westward the lonely Moor extends for mile after undulating mile intersected by hidden combes and torrents, 'wild, little cultivated, bleak and lonely', but not deserted, for here the Exmoor ponies graze. If you leave Dunkery and set off across the Moor, perhaps other presences may accompany you, for the rough tracks will lead you into places now solitary but once visited by vanished peoples and still marked, in standing stones and barrows, with memorials of our nameless but not forgotten predecessors.

The majesty of this panorama is complemented by the delicacy and homeliness of the scene near at hand, described many years ago as 'neither colossal, nor overwhelming, (but) infinitely beautiful and picturesque'. The hillside north of Dunkery falls away steeply for many hundreds of feet into the sea of foliage which fills the wooded combes of Horner Water and its tributaries. Over to the left, hidden on the seaward side of the hills, stands the lonely farmhouse to which Coleridge came and where Kubla Khan emerged from a dream into the light. In the middle distance the fertile Vale of Porlock, with fields as neat as gardens, runs from the sea and marshlands of Porlock Weir eastward to join the hidden valley of the River Avill, which flows through the beautiful villages of Timberscombe and Dunster. On the other side of the Vale, Bossington Hill and North Hill rise almost vertically, and Selworthy church gleams white on its terrace above the picturesque village green and the tree-shaded lane.

Further yet to the east, beyond where North Hill drops precipitously to the sea and Minehead lies hidden, Dunster marshes, the only mile square of level land in all West Somerset, show a carpet of green; and a moving column of smoke and steam announces the West Somerset Railway. If it should be thought that the twentieth century, so pervasive in every other place, has passed by this secluded district, look again at the levels of Dunster; ten miles beyond, you will see, like some massive fortress, the nuclear reactors of Hinkley Point.

History, then, has not left this corner of England

Heath and furze on Hopcott Common, looking toward Minehead and the coast of South Wales.

completely neglected. Invaders and ravagers have come: Norse pirates from Brittany in 918, Danish and Viking raiders, the exiled Harold Godwinsson in 1052, Cavaliers and Roundheads, the Doones, Judge Jeffreys' hangmen, the flood waters of 1952, and more frequent than all in the earlier centuries, and more feared, the plague. But these incursions were but interruptions of the more genuine history, the often unwritten account of the toil and husbandry which have brought both the fertile valley and the unfruitful wilderness into the service of man.

But how that came about, how a wasteland became a national park, a place of re-creation, will take some time to tell.

Looking toward Leighland and the distant sea from Sticklepath, Brendon Hill.

1 The making of Exmoor

Every national park is unique in its beauty. Indeed, beauty and uniqueness combined may be said to have prompted the conception and designation of each individual park. Exmoor's uniqueness, Exmoor's virtue, Exmoor's peculiar charm, are more subtle and more difficult to identify, except that in her are blended the beauties of all the other national parks (except, maybe, the Lake District and Snowdonia) yet with no characteristic to excess. Her 265 square miles contain high sandstone cliffs as majestic as any in England, but humanized, so to speak, by the sea at their foot and the heather-clad hills around; romantic chasms and wooded gorges. Robert Southey wrote of the wooded gorge at Lynmouth as 'the most beautiful and picturesque I have seen, except perhaps for Cintra, in all Europe'.

The West Lyn gorge, near Lynmouth.

Foreland Point, northernmost point of the Exmoor coast.

Exmoor has moorlands like those of Dartmoor but without the forbidding tors; expanses wide and unfrequented enough, seemingly, for a traveller to be lost to human knowledge for months and years, yet nowhere more than five miles distant from habitation if the way is known. Its valleys are precipitous enough to send an incautious walker headlong, yet not so deep that half an hour's exertion will not bring you up again to the wide, windy moor.

And the waters of Exmoor – the Heddon, Lyn, Chetsford Water, Avill, Luxborough Brook, Haddeo, Danes Brook, Kinsford Water, Yeo, Mole and Bray, together with the Exe and Barle – ripple and plash over the flat, iron-tinged stones southward to the Channel or north to the Severn sea; singing in summer an indefinable song, but in winter rushing down through woodlands to the sea in cascade after cascade – and like mountain streams everywhere, subject to surging floods that can sweep men, beasts and buildings to destruction. Here are types of beauty, changing from moment to moment but everlastingly the same, which might, at first sight, be found in any mountainous region – but on closer acquaintance you will find them unique; different in nature and configuration from even their near neighbours on Dartmoor. The difference derives from the more *intimate* scale of Exmoor, from the more moderate altitude, and the underlying rocks of the region where the 'waters' rise and the steep-sided combes and valleys through which they make their way to the sea.

Despite the proverb, beauty *is* more than skin deep. It is bred in the bone, it takes its form from the

Opposite above Map of Exmoor showing the river systems.

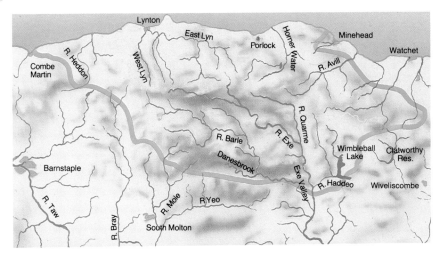

The Barle at Dulverton.

underlying structure, whether of the human face or of the landscape. It is the underlying rock formations of a region, subjected to the stress and wear of eons of geological time, that impart a characteristic beauty to such widely differing land forms as the craggy peaks of the Lake District, the mountains of the Brecon Beacons, the 'scars' of the North Yorkshire Moors – and the tableland of Exmoor.

The River Barle in South Barton Wood, Hawkridge.

The term 'tableland' used of Exmoor is an over-simplification, though you might well have the impression of a plateau if you were transported blindfold to the heart of the Moor and there caught your first glimpse of mile upon mile of grassland gently undulating toward the distant elevation of Dunkery or Shoulsbury. The appearance is deceptive, and Richard Jefferies, who in a brief visit absorbed as much of the spirit of the Moor as a lesser naturalist might do in a lifetime, wrote:

'The moors of the Exe river are not flat stretches of marshland, but hills of great height covered with heather. The term mountains may almost be applied to them . . . but the conformation of the country is such that on entering it the elevations do not seem very unusual, for as it is all high and raised the eye has nothing with which to contrast it. When on the moor it appears an immense table-land, intersected by deep narrow valleys, called combes, at the bottom of which a stream always flows. At some distance apart are ranges of hills rising gradually and with gentle slopes above the general level of the moors. The curves appear so moderate and the ascent so easy that there can be no difficulty in walking or riding over them. . . . But on going towards them, the table-land suddenly sinks in a deep combe, when it is apparent that the moor which looked so level is really the top of a hill. This combe has to be descended, and ascended, and the sides are high and steep. Presently another combe intervenes, and after five miles' walking very little progress has been made. . . . The country is, in fact, very deceptive, much wider, and much more difficult than it looks.'

The great upland region of Exmoor, then, together with its eastern outrider, the Brendon Hills, is intersected by numberless valleys and combes, through which run streams and 'waters' which, except in the far north and west, all flow into the River Exe. All valleys, in every landscape, have been formed by the action of the weather over countless ages of prehistory. The wind, rain and ice have worn away softer rock from a hard core, and diminished the core itself, and the resultant streams have formed ever deepening valleys, their depth and steepness varying, in general, in proportion to their age and the hardness of the surrounding rock.

Lynton and Lynmouth, looking west from Countisbury Hill.

Where the mountains are, in geological terms, young they stand high and proud; where old and time-wasted, they form no more than protuberances, convexities and elevations. Exmoor, though 'younger' in geological terms than 'shield' areas such as the Lizard, is as old as most of Cornwall and Devon – that is, immensely old.

The geological map shows Exmoor as almost entirely made up of Devonian rocks, including slates, grits and sandstones originally formed of mud and sand which were deposited 350 million years ago on the bed of a primeval ocean. Then a monstrous but unimaginably gradual upheaval forced up the earth's crust, tilting and folding the strata and forming, under pressure, the mass of rock that was to become Exmoor. The mud, under pressure also, became the slate beds which now extend from the western sea to the south-eastern

Geological map of Exmoor.

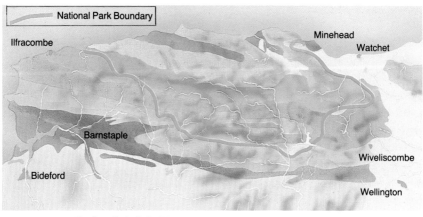

National Park Boundary

Ilfracombe

Minehead

Watchet

Barnstaple

Wiveliscombe

Bideford

Wellington

Rock Type	Age in Million Years	Geological period	Method of Formation
Peat Boulder Clay	1.8	Recent & Pleistocene	Dead vegetation in bog or marsh. River and lake deposits.
Limestone Shale	135 240	Jurassic and Triassic	Deposits in shallow sea.
Limestone Sandstone	280	Carboniferous	Deposition of various sediments in river deltas and coastal lagoons.
Shale Slate Sandstone	350		Deposition of various sediments in river deltas and sea.
Sandstone Slate		Devonian	Deposits in river deltas and coastal lagoons.
Sandstone Tuff			Deposits of coarse sediments at river mouth – dust from volcanic eruptions.
Slate			Deposits in shallow sea and altered by pressure.
Grit Shale Limestone			Deposits of sediment and coral reef organisms in shallow sea.
Sandstone Grit			Deposits from desert shore to river mouth and shallow sea.
Sandstone Slate	415		Deposits in shallow sea becoming shallower.

Terminal curvature in Hangman Grits at Scob Hill, Brendon. The rock takes its name from Great Hangman, Combe Martin, where it most notably extrudes. The meaning of 'Hangman' is not the obvious one of a place of execution but probably 'old stone'.

edge of the Brendon Hills. The Devonian formation contains iron ore which was profitably mined, and the slate of the Brendon Hills was quarried for hundreds of years.

Looked at in section, Exmoor today would appear almost wedge-shaped, its northern cliffs rising steeply from the sea to more than 1,500 feet, from where its surface descends almost imperceptibly until it merges with the hills of mid-Devon. In the north east and east the precipitous escarpment of the Brendon Hills leads down to regions, respectively, of Red Marls and New Red Sandstone, and here the streams have made a delightful landscape of sheltered combes and winding valleys leading to a rich alluvial plain. But it is Exmoor's coastline which is particularly distinguished by its hog's back cliffs. These have a long, steep fall towards the coast with only the last part of the cliff falling sheer down to the sea, unlike most of England's flat-topped cliffs.

Exmoor, in its 'unimproved' state, has two kinds of soil. Down in the valleys the good soil is loamy on top and clayey below and drains rapidly. It lacks lime but can be made fertile with heavy dressings. The upland soil, however, is poor, peaty and wet, and it sustains chiefly heather – which of course is a constituent of peat. In the layers below the peat there lies a thin iron and clay 'pan', impermeable to water, and until this 'pan' is broken by deep ploughing the surface remains waterlogged, recalcitrant and unproductive.

The three major ice sheets which for many thousands of years overlay much of the northern hemisphere never extended quite as far south as these latitudes; but as recently as perhaps 20,000 years ago the last ice sheet came quite close. Although not glaciated as such, in winter Exmoor was covered in deep ice and snow, and with each summer's thaw the dislodged topsoil, stones and sludge would slide a little further downhill, slipping on the permanently frozen ground beneath. In some places, at high altitudes, these movements formed parallel ridges along the slopes. They might be taken for strip lynchets, the terraces of medieval cultivation, but they date from thousands of years before man came to settle on Exmoor.

During these millennia there was probably always some plant life on Exmoor, but no doubt the plant cover contracted or expanded with successive advances and retreats of the ice. By about 12000 BC the ice had begun its long and – up to the present – final withdrawal, and growing conditions improved. For many years, however, the continental-sized ice sheets continued to hold so much water that the level of the sea lay 100 feet or more below the present one, so that Britain, to give it its modern

The Valley of Rocks, Lynton, is thought to have been the outlet long ago of the Lyn to the sea. When the waves wore away the comparatively weak rocks between the Lyn and the sea, the river took the direct way out, leaving the Valley of Rocks high and dry and continuing to wear away its bed from 500 feet above sea level to the present one.

The floor of the Valley of Rocks has filled with 'head', a deposit of sandstone and slate set in clay and caused by climatic conditions near a glacial margin. Summer thaw brought down weathered bedrock material, but the salt water could not penetrate the permafrost. The bedrock materials became mixed to form a homogeneous 'head' deposit.

name, was not an island but a prolongation of the mainland of 'Europe'. The 'Bristol Channel' was the shallow valley of a great river running west to east, and the north west coast of 'Exmoor' followed a line roughly from the present Ilfracombe to Swansea.

Present land

Land in 5000 B.C.

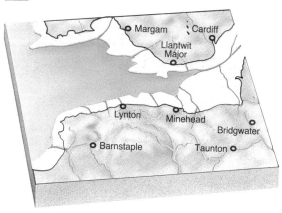

The coastline of Exmoor and South Wales, 5000 BC.

'All things flow,' said the old Greek; the whole of nature exists in a state of continual change. As the ice sheets melted, the north of 'Britain', freed from their weight, rose and the south sank, like a tellurian seesaw. About the year 7500 BC the sea broke through the 'Straits of Dover' and 'Britain' became an island. By about 5000 BC the waters in the 'Bristol Channel' had risen to around thirty feet below the present level and formed a coastline recognizably, if not closely, similar in outline to that of today.

Even before this, forest was already forming two hundred miles to the south and plant seeds, brought by the wind or in birds' droppings, were taking the place of the retreating tundra. First came dwarf willows and birches, but with a warmer climate the larger birches and 'Scots' pine followed, giving shelter for other trees, particularly hazel, to spread, with much alder in marshy places and oak and lime on the slopes and in the combes.

The evidence for this evolution in the days before recorded history comes from analyses of pollen taken from peat and dated partly by a painstaking consideration of the rate at which peat is formed and the depth from which the pollen has been taken, and partly by the measurement of the radio carbon

Woodland near Wimbleball.

content, checked and modified by a process known as 'calibration'. Such dates can only be approximate, but they suggest interesting facts: that by about 6000 BC the climate was moist and warm, and broad-leaved trees such as oak, alder, lime and elm flourished alongside the pine and hazel and perhaps supplanted them in the more favoured areas. Then a little after 3700 BC came a drier, sunnier, golden time which lasted for 2,000 years. Around 1500 BC the climate worsened, and not until about 200 BC did it settle into the pattern we know today – subject to marine influences, with brusque alternation of driving rain and vivifying sun, with buffeting south westerlies which stunt the few trees on high ground; a climate wayward and unpredictable, but which for two thousand years has dictated what shall or shall not grow or be grown on Exmoor.

The altitude of the Moor makes it unlikely that, even 5,000 years ago, the forest which covered much of it contained oaks and elms as majestic as those down in the valleys, but undoubtedly they grew here in great numbers, and these alder, oak, elm and lime trees may be thought of as the natural vegetation of Exmoor before man made any significant impression on it. (Tree stumps, known as bog-oak, have been found in peat diggings on Exmoor even as high as 1,300 feet). The change of climate alone does not account for their disappearance. Man took a meddlesome hand.

2 **Early man on the Moor**

Man may have frequented Exmoor – to use the modern name – in the later of the periods between the Ice Ages, but no evidence has been found here to support this conjecture, and not till long after the last ice sheets receded did conditions favour permanent occupation. Palaeolithic and Mesolithic (Old and Middle Stone Age) man may have wandered over the district, hunting, fishing and snaring game; Mesolithic man left traces of his activities in the forms of small stone arrowheads, scrapers and cutting blades. He may have settled in a few locations on and around the Moor, certainly at Hawkcombe Head (844457), but the artefacts discovered so far are the tools of nomads; these people had not yet learnt settled agriculture. That epochal advance came with the Neolithic (New Stone) Age, 'characterized', in the words of L V Grinsell; 'by predominantly long-headed immigrants who introduced primitive pasture and agriculture and were potters', though of course they went on hunting, fishing and gathering food. They left little trace of their domesticity, for Exmoor lacked massive, durable boulders, and the timber and ragstone they would have used for building soon fell back into the earth. Enough of their artifacts have been found in a concentration on Kentisbury Down to suggest that they occupied the site for a long time, but they did not push on into the Moor. The most important evidence of occupation is an earthwork on Parracombe Common (692448), a circular earth bank about 120 feet across with a ditch on the inside, and another on Longstone Allotments (707427). They are probably 'henge' monuments – centres for ceremony and worship unique on Exmoor but similar to 'henges' in Mendip and Cornwall.

Even in those remote days, however, Exmoor was apparently serving as a refuge for one after another of the peoples who, from 2500 to 900 BC, spread across the country from east to west and from south to west and north, only to be harried and pushed on by others in turn. Yet they may often have intermingled with the older inhabitants rather than exterminated them.

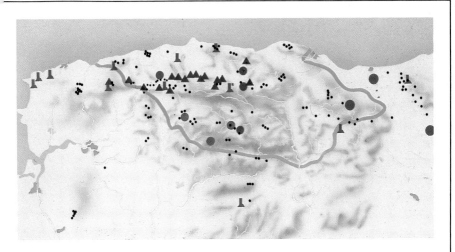

● Stone circle

▲ Stone setting

⚓ Standing stone

. Round barrow

● Bell barrow

● Disc barrow

● Bronze implement hoard

〰 National Park boundary

Bronze Age sites in the
Exmoor area.

Around 2500 BC immigrants introduced finely-
made pottery vessels which we know as beakers,
and their makers are known, obviously, as the
Beaker folk. About the same time, 'copper
implements were introduced, followed slightly later
by the discovery of the art of alloying copper with
tin to produce bronze, and the introduction of the
simpler types of implement of this material' (L V
Grinsell). These people 'practised body burial in
the contracted posture often beneath small round
barrows'. Certainly the Stone and Bronze Age
cultures existed side by side, and Neolithic man in
general would welcome the new bronze
implements while perforce making do with the old
until the new became more plentiful.

Bronze Age men, with a more advanced culture,
saw the moor in a different light from their Neolithic
predecessors. With the advent of a drier climate it
was becoming ripe for settlement, and they settled,
and left, as Charles Whybrow phrased it, 'their
impress for ever on the windy heights where they
built their round barrows'. Enough of these remain –
three or four hundred, with numerous stone double-
alignments and circles – to prove that these people
formed a large and organized population.

The Neolithic and Bronze Age cultures merged,
and the tribes of Exmoor and the West generally

seem to have lived at peace with one another, possibly because there was room for all. Around 600 BC the first iron users arrived, but in small enough numbers to be assimilated by the existing tribes and cultures, and over the next few generations the superiority of their implements brought the inhabitants into the Iron Age. But iron meant more efficient weapons as well as tools. Both Bronze and Iron Age men were constrained to build hillforts, and these remained in occupation right through to the Roman invasion.

They were needed. Shortly after 300 BC the Celts invaded Britain, armed with iron weapons which made them all but irresistible. This is not to imply that they came in overwhelming strength. More probably, like the Angles and Saxons 700 and 800 years later, they came in small bands, occupied the land they needed – which involved the dispossession but not necessarily the extermination of the inhabitants – and settled down from a warrior to a farming life. But by the year 55 BC, when Britain first came within the scope of written history, 'the lands along the south coast . . . were thickly studded with homesteads, and corn, cattle and timber were plentiful.' By this time, however, the weather on

Cow Castle on the Barle below Simonsbath and an Iron Age fort guarding the approach from the lowlands.

Exmoor had changed for the worse. A 'sub-Atlantic' phase had begun about 850 BC, with much wetter and cooler summers, and lasted for almost a thousand years. The inhabitants of the south coast, living in reasonable comfort and enjoying the advantages of trade with Roman Gaul, would not be tempted overmuch to venture up on to the bleak highlands. Nevertheless, some fear or necessity prompted the hillmen to build 'forts', though whether these were for permanent habitation or for use only in times of danger is not yet known. Perhaps in due course archaeology will tell us why.

Certainly, nearly everything of ancient structure on Exmoor dates from these prehistoric times. The most impressive of these monuments, mysterious and boding for some observers, are the fifty or sixty great skyline burial barrows – 'burrows' in local parlance – with their characteristic forms of 'bowl', like an inverted pudding-basin; 'bell', a bowl with a narrow rim round the base, and 'disc', a platform very little above ground level, with a surrounding ditch or bank or both. Few of them are wholly intact, for grave-robbers have dug into them and left a depression at the centre of each, but they remain impressive as monuments of the industry of a

Iron Age sites in the Exmoor area.

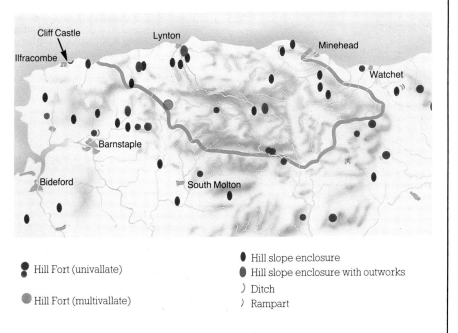

Cliff Castle	Lynton
Ilfracombe	Minehead
	Watchet
Barnstaple	
Bideford	South Molton

● Hill slope enclosure
◐ Hill slope enclosure with outworks
) Ditch
) Rampart

Hill Fort (univallate)

Hill Fort (multivallate)

scattered but organized population more than three thousand years ago. Comparison with barrows in Wiltshire dates them to the peak of Bronze Age civilization about 1800 BC. 'The best line of them' (Eardley-Wilmot) 'curves for two miles along the south-west ridge of the moor, from Setta Barrow (sadly mutilated by an "improver"), through the high cluster of Five Barrows, to Two Barrows, and on to the small One Barrow at the eastern end of the ridge, about a quarter of a mile north of the county boundary road. There are more than twenty altogether, including bowl, bell and several kinds of disc', and no two of them are exactly alike.

A general guide such as this cannot catalogue the profusion of standing stones, stone rows and alignments, circles, earthworks, forts, stells, quincunxes and boundary stones which are scattered across the Moor at apparent random, but more probably in a series of patterns that imaginative archaeology may perhaps one day reveal. If they interest you, you will find them described in detail, with their conjectured purposes, in the admirable studies mentioned in the Bibliography at the end of this book.

The Romans, in their four centuries of occupation

Dunkery.

Longstone and Longstone Barrow; probably a Bronze Age standing stone, $9\frac{1}{2}$ feet high. Some standing stones are fairly modern scratching posts for animals.

Shoulsbarrow (more properly Shoulsbury), above the Bray valley.

Below
The Caratacus Stone, on Winsford Hill, was noted as a Forest boundary mark as long ago as 1219 The inscription in Latin letters, not Celtic, dates from the Dark Ages, probably the sixth century, but the stone may have stood here much longer and was perhaps originally erected as a Bronze Age head-of-stream sacred stone.

of Britain, made little impact on Exmoor apart from establishing two small forts or signal stations on the north coast at Old Burrow and Martinhoe, to keep watch on the unconquered Silures of South Wales, and possibly the fort at Shoulsbury and some mining of the iron ore deposits. Nevertheless, the knowledge of their presence was sufficient to keep the tribes in awe and confine their turbulent spirits to inter-tribal brawls. In time Roman culture made its mark strongly enough to persist into the Dark Ages, as demonstrated by the Caratacus Stone on Winsford Hill, on which the words CARATACI NEPVS, 'Kinsman of Caratacus' are inscribed in Roman letters, not Celtic.

3 **The Forest**

For almost three centuries after the Romans
withdrew from Britain to defend their heartland
against the barbarians, Exmoor remained
comparatively undisturbed from without, however
much the inhabitants may have quarreled with one
another! The Anglo-Saxons, invading Britain as
warrior-farmers, kept on their fighting role no
longer than needed to carve out land to settle on and
get on with the business of living. But during this
time another invasion of Exmoor was taking place,
carried out by a handful of men over a long period –
the conversion of the Exmoor people to Christianity
by missionaries of the Celtic church from Wales,
some of whose names are commemorated in the
dedications of the churches at Culbone (Beuno),
Porlock (Dubricius – Dyfrig), Timberscombe
(Petroc), Carhampton (Carantoc), and – just outside

Heart of the Lorna Doone
country.

Exmoor – Watchet (Decuman). The inscribed Caratacus Stone on Winsford Hill, the Wheeled Cross Stone at Culbone, and the Cavudus Stone near Lynton all date from this time.

Not until AD 710, when King Ine of Wessex defeated the British and set up his fortress at Taunton, did the Saxons come near the Moor in any numbers. Some then moved north west from Taunton and settled in the valleys of West Somerset – at Oare (the very name means 'boundary'), Culbone, Porlock, Cutcombe, Exford, Winsford and Dulverton; others came north from Exeter and south Devon and settled in the valleys at Brendon, Countisbury, Lynton, Parracombe, Challacombe, Twitchen and the Ansteys. As cautious farmers, they knew better than to venture their livelihood on the heavy soils and in the driving rains of the high moor. Upland Exmoor, if not already deserted, became so.

Deserted, but not untraversed. By the ninth century the Anglo-Saxons had been in the country for three or four hundred years, had mingled with the British to become the English and had evolved from warrior-settlers into settled, peaceable farmers. But the onslaught of the Danes and the conquest of the larger part of England put their freedom and modest well-being in peril, even in this remote corner of Wessex (if indeed Wessex came so far). The Danish attack culminated in the retreat of King Alfred to the Isle of Athelney. The territorial army, called the 'fyrd', and the men of Devon, Somerset, Wiltshire and Hampshire rallied to support Alfred and defeated the invaders at Ethandune. It was supposedly to aid such rallying in times of national danger that the 'harepath' or army track was built.

An impressive memorial to our forefathers' ability to organize the human resources of a region for a common purpose, the harepath ran – and long stretches of it remain clearly visible today – from the Midlands through Gloucester and Bristol and thence, by secret trackways through the marshes, to the River Parrett, which it crossed at or near Combwich; from here it climbed over the Quantocks and on over the ridge of the Brendons to Exford and Simonsbath, and thence to Barnstaple and Cornwall. Yet the path almost certainly dates back further than the Danish wars, and 'army path' no more implies exclusive use than does 'Royal Mail' or 'Queen's highway'. No one has formed an estimate of its age, but that indefinable, yet almost tangible, feeling of extreme age hovers around it,

The line of the harepath is shown with striking clarity in this stretch near Heath Poult Cress.

and SHBurton had an experience which he could not explain or yet discount. On a louring April day he was unknowingly following the track near Mole's Chamber when an overwhelming sense of antiquity gripped him. He walked slowly on but was no longer alone. He had no clear idea of where he was in time, but shadowy figures moved down the track with him, their backs bent beneath great bundles, and kept company with him until his boots rang on the metalled surface of the main road. Strange, inexplicable happenings take place on the Moor, but rarely do they so revealingly draw aside the curtain of the dark.

But even if armed men moved over the Moor, no battles were fought. The northern margin, as noted earlier, witnessed attacks by Danish pirates on Watchet in 918, 977, 988 and 997 and on Porlock in 918 and 988, and a raid by Harold Godwinsson on Porlock Bay in 1052, but otherwise history passed it by. Yet quiet events were going on. By Saxon custom, unappropriated land could be parcelled out by the king to his followers. Gradually, as the power of the kings grew, this land became part of their demesne and the old rights of the nation over it

Mole's Chamber, a lonely and formerly dangerous part of the Moor.

were lost. This happened with Exmoor. But on the other hand, Saxon settlers in the villages were establishing by usage rights of 'commons' on the moor; digging peat, foraging for fuel and turning out their cattle for summer grazing.

As the population and dwellings increased, the forests were cleared and the wolves and 'such like ravenous beasts' which had sheltered in them were destroyed. This left the field clear for the 'beasts of pleasure as well as delicate meat' – especially the deer. 'The kings of this land began to be careful for the preservation of them, and in order thereto to privilege certain woods and places so that no man may hurt or destroy them there; and thus the said places became Forests.'

The word needs explanation. In its old meaning 'forest' did not imply trees but simply a district where deer and certain other animals were reserved for the king and protected from his people by Forest Law (from Norman days onward). The district might be wooded, but that was incidental. At some time before the Norman Conquest, the heart of Exmoor became such a Royal Forest and probably included the whole of the great wilderness extending from Porlock to Bray and from Martinhoe to Dulverton. From early in the thirteenth century the western and southern boundaries of the Forest were accepted as the boundary of Somerset and Devon. As far as is known, none of the kings or queens between 1066 and the Civil War came hunting on Exmoor, but the Forest had its complement of Warden or Chief Forester, woodwards, verderers, regarders and foresters, the latter acting as gamekeepers – more often than not unpaid, and therefore recouping themselves by impounding the cattle of the Forest dwellers, making false charges and generally thriving upon a well-organized system of blackmail and extortion. In the early days the harsh Forest Laws were rigidly enforced, but after 1301, when Edward I disafforested the eastern part, Forest Law decayed. By Tudor times the local gentry, their friends and servants were hunting the deer and keeping hounds, but with the outbreak of the Civil War in 1642 regular stag hunting on Exmoor ceased, and was not revived till a hundred years later. As for the irregular kind, who knows!

To catalogue the six centuries of Wardens would be wearisome, but one of them must be mentioned by name, a singularly rich character, James Boevey. In 1649 the House of Commons, having disposed of

the king, logically decided to dispose of all royal property as well. A survey of Exmoor was carried out in 1651, and soon after this James Boevey purchased the freehold of Exmoor and the Forest passed out of the possession of the crown.

Boevey was of Dutch ancestry, as his name suggests; a wealthy merchant who left off trading at thirty-two and withdrew to the country, 'the aire of the citie not agreeing with him'. He counteracted his indifferent health by constant activity, and he

The Forest and county boundary fence at Broad Mead.

radiated mental energy. He also wrote thirty-two books and spoke eight languages.

None of these accomplishments would have helped him on Exmoor, but right at the outset of his wardenship he broke with tradition and showed a personal interest. Almost his first act was to build Simonsbath House, where you may see the date of completion, 1654, carved in one of the beams, and where, incidentally, you may browse to satiety and slumber in a comfort which would have caused the founder to rub his 'sprightly hazel eie' in disbelief.

James Boevey enjoyed a temperament which delighted in contest, litigation and the making of enemies, and for twenty-six years of his forty-three year tenure he was engaged on and off in litigation against the rights of the Free Suitors and the Suitors at Large. He lost in the end, but in the meantime he had obtained a judgement from the Courts that the Warden had the right to fix the rates for grazing, his chief source of income, at whatever level he chose. He survived the Restoration unscathed, skilfully negotiating a lease as Crown tenant with the new owner, the Marquess of Ormond, who had managed to obtain letters patent within two months after Charles II's return, whereas scores of faithful Cavaliers fretted their lives away in vain and

Simonsbath House, built by James Boevey as his great house in the mid-seventeenth century, now an hotel.

diminishing expectation of deserved recompense.

In the second half of the eighteenth century the wardenship went to three successive Sir Thomas Dyke Aclands. They revived stag hunting and improved the breed of Exmoor ponies, strengthening the stock. But when in 1814 their regime ended and a new phase in the life of Exmoor began, it was clearly seen that all the centuries since the Dark Ages and the Norman Conquest had left the face of the Moor virtually unscarred and unchanged. Scattered sites showed traces of mining, and at Simonsbath Boevey's house, now the home of the deputy forester, stood in a hundred acres of reclaimed land; but everywhere else the Forest and the high moor preserved its immemorial visage, treeless, heather-clad, and deserted by man.

4 **The village**

So wild was Exmoor, so unsuited to any other enterprise apart from grazing sheep and rounding up the 'equas silvestras' (wild horses), that we almost inevitably form the impression that farming, even in the foothills and valleys, was a hand-to-mouth affair. And no doubt it was, but the condition was general, and there is no reason to believe that famine and bad harvests and the recurrent outbreaks of blight, mildew, smut, foot-rot, liver fluke and murrain wrought more destruction here than elsewhere in England. In Saxon days the farmers of the southern approaches were pushing the boundaries of their enclosed land up the hillsides, and recent checks by plant-counting techniques have provided strong evidence, backed by pre-1066 documents, that some of the field hedges west of Bratton Fleming are at least a thousand years old.

Exford today, with a village green in the centre.

Whether these Saxons founded the holdings themselves or dispossessed other holders we cannot tell, but the fact remains that when in 1086 William I sent down his carrion-crow clerics to pry into the land tenures, they confirmed the existence of some fifty-five manors, great and small, on the perimeter of the Moor; and by about the year 1300, before the Black Death struck, over 130 farms were working.

The dispersion of these farms across the countryside, by contrast to the Saxon practice in some lowland areas of a village surrounded by great fields, was of course dictated by the broken landscape; but at some stage, responding to the need for social concourse and the diversification and specialization of labour, certain of the manors, rather than the farms, in favoured circumstances developed into villages: at Asseford or Exford, for instance, a meeting place of the harepath and moorland tracks; at Winesford or Winsford; at Dolvertune or Dulverton, where the River Barle emerged into the more populous lowland and a market could be held; at Widipol or Withypool, Lolochesberie or Luxborough, Brandone or Brendon, well-watered valleys sheltering houses from the upland storms. In each of these, and in the sterner hill settlements of Withiglea (Withiel Florey), Codecoma (Cutcombe), Brunetone (Kingsbrompton) and Burneton (Brompton Ralph), the men of the twelfth, thirteenth and fourteenth centuries built plain, sturdy churches.

Otherwise the villages probably changed little in appearance until well into the nineteenth century. Some cottages and farmhouses were enlarged and their roof trees were raised, but Exmoor, remote from the developing areas of manufacturing and with primitive communications, derived only a meagre and delayed benefit from the Industrial Revolution.

This is not to say that Exmoor folk in Regency days led lives as spartan as their forefathers', but outsiders undoubtedly looked on them as dragging behind the times and as butts for urban wit. Yet the knowledge and ignorance, poverty and wealth, were less extreme than in the cities, and Exmoor still preserved certain virtues once common in country life but becoming submerged under the human tide of the towns. The people were individualistic, hospitable and tough.

'I liked those times', wrote a Victorian parson. 'There were two worlds in those days, the world of what men call civilization . . . and the world of the country, in which you could preserve some sort of individuality, and think and be quiet.

'In the country there were many people of a high order of intelligence . . . and in country libraries there were books of a much higher character than most of those which are popular today [the end of the nineteenth century].

'Everybody was hospitable. No one ever begrudged you anything. You could eat, drink, sleep, shoot, fish, ride, or walk almost anywhere you pleased, and the pleasure afforded by your company was thought to be payment enough. The truth is that the country was not at that time opened up, and people were glad of the companionship of anyone who was a little different from themselves.'

Nevertheless, in the first half of the nineteenth century the villages did develop, even if very gradually, and the history of Exford may point to what happened elsewhere.

At the beginning of the century the parish contained fifty-six dwellings but no real centre. Half the parish consisted of wild open moor, the other half scattered farms. The church stood alone on a hill above the village, perhaps on some long-forgotten sacred site, with the rectory nearby. There was no village as such, and even the traditional manor house was lacking. This, however, had the happy result that the farmers, mostly yeomen with security of tenure if not of livelihood, were independent and self-reliant and by dint of hard work, and even harder work by their labourers, made a passable living. At any rate, the more intelligent and enterprising did, if they farmed 200 to 300 acres. But another class, even less favoured by nature, had to struggle:

'[The] farming tenantry of the district rent or otherwise occupy from 200 to 300 acres of land, the greater part of which is subject to a system of up-and-down husbandry, and to which is generally attached a small proportion of permanent pasture, and of marsh or meadow-land. . . . There is a second class of farmer, who are found to labour hard, and for very little profit. The class of farmers first mentioned, may be said to have most of the comfort and conveniences of life about them; they are generally owners of trips or small flocks of sheep, depastured upon

Exmoor, and of the cows and bullocks summered upon the moors and other grass-grounds in the occupation of their poorer neighbours, who, destitute of the means of stocking their farms, are obliged to resort . . . to agistment stock, for the consumption of their herbage. . . . Cleanliness (at least in their homes) seems little attended to, and, though sparing and frugal in all their domestic affairs, they are but seldom regarded as a thriving people, or considered to be in any way improving that very small capital with which they began the world.'

Thus, with a doubtful shake of the head, Charles Vancouver wrote in 1808, but at that time the inaccessibility of the heart of the Moor, the complete lack of available capital, the French war and the illiteracy and ingrained conservatism all combined to keep Exford in a state of backwardness. In 1818 came the moment for change, when, as will be recounted presently, a Worcestershire ironmaster, John Knight, set to work to bridle and tame the Moor. Farm workers, craftsmen and tradesmen arrived, and as their number grew the air of Simonsbath, five miles west of Exford, hummed with 'improvement'. Those who came from up country had of course to pass through Exford, and no doubt the parish could have benefited almost immediately; but as living examples of the Somerset saying, 'We can be led but we 'on't be druv,' the Exford farmers bided their time. No one was going to stampede them into bettering their condition. Let someone show the way and they might follow. Or not.

In 1823, the fourth year of Knight's activity, when reclamation was getting into its stride, the man for Exford appeared. The rectorship of Exford fell vacant and the patron, Peterhouse College, offered the living to one of its Fellows, the Reverend Joseph Relph.

Relph was born in Cumberland in 1784, the son of a 'statesman', a small landowner farming his own estate. He and Exford suited each other. He possessed the necessary knowledge and conscientiousness toward his pastorate, and that made him a man of mark; but he also brought north country tenacity and hard-headedness and, perhaps most important of all, the knowledge and interests of a hill farmer. His neighbour at Simonsbath many years later described him as 'a good man with a good wife' – the lady spoke as broad a dialect as

Exford church, enlarged by Parson Relph.

himself – 'but of a primitive, completely bucolic type not often met with in the Church. He was as great with his woolly flock as with his parishoners.' Such was the man who at the age of thirty-nine began to 'guide the sleepy and self-centred parish of Exford into a new age of industry and prosperity.' (MFreeman-Archer)

He rebuilt the rectory at his own expense, planted hedgerows and made plantations about the house, 'altogether in good taste', and with the help of one labourer, stocked his glebeland and set it in good order. But Exford still lacked a good road to the outside world, and less than three pounds had been spent on Exford highways in the past twenty years. Relph called vestry meetings to persuade the farmers to co-operate and fixed a highway rate of sixpence in the pound, and in 1827 the vestry decided to let a stretch of road to him for twenty-four pounds, which he sublet into smaller parts to be made up. Work on the roads started at the river by the ford and gradually spread all along the tracks leading from them and connecting, on the Simonsbath side, with the new road built by Knight; but the whole project took Relph more than thirty years, until 1859.

Other improvements, however, came almost immediately. The White Horse was rebuilt in the very first years and another inn, the Crown, was added. Then Knight's agent, Osmond Lock, built a row of five houses in the centre of the village to accommodate the new workmen and their wives and children, with shops for a carpenter and a blacksmith. Gradually a nucleated village came into being, and the fifty-six houses in the parish in 1811 had almost doubled by the census year of 1851, and the population had risen from 316 to 580. Half the children in the parish – thirty of each sex – were being taught in two dames' schools, and the relief of the poor and the Poor House were being funded on a complicated but workable system by which the mill and outbuildings which formed the basis of the local charity were completely rebuilt, money was borrowed at interest, the poor received their gifts, the interest was paid annually and the capital gradually repaid. The enclosure of common land had made the lot of the poor even more miserable, and in the mid-1840s the failure of the potato crop for two successive years brought them to the edge of starvation; but such distress was widespread. In other respects Exford had become a village and centre of a moorland parish, complete with church, chapel, a fine stone bridge, schools, shops, inns and the workplaces of craftsmen and tradesmen who provided for every daily need.

But while the village developed, the Moor itself also underwent a profound change, and we will now return to its story at the point where we left it; immemorial, treeless, heather-clad and deserted by man.

5 The Knights of Exmoor

It was the treelessness of Exmoor that eventually provoked the most momentous change in its landscape. In the year 1810 Napoleon and his adopted nation seemed to have taken a rest from reducing the population of Europe to a governable number, largely because they had crushed resistance everywhere on the mainland except in Spain. But the respite did not deceive Parliament. They knew that only the Navy had preserved the kingdom from conquest, and they knew also that shipbuilders, housebuilders and ironmasters had used up at a dangerous rate the raw material of the Navy's men-o'-war, the English oak. So they uncharacteristically insisted on the Crown lands and forests being managed for the public good and in particular to yield timber for the Navy. Some of the very finest oaks in the country grew in Nettlecombe

The oaks of Nettlecombe, many of them planted in the early seventeenth century, are now past their prime, but enough of them remain to confirm the old reputation.

Park, on the northern slopes of the Brendon Hills; mature, sound-timbered trees valued at 100 guineas or £105 each – perhaps almost £3,000 in terms of the 1980s – and Sir John Trevelyan had accepted an offer of £30,000 (or almost £1 million) for them. The day arrived for them to be felled – or 'throwed', in local parlance. Sir John heard that the men had arrived prepared for the slaughter and straightway he drove up in his pony carriage and chased them out of the park. But when Sir Thomas Acland applied to the Surveyor General of Land Revenue for a new lease four years' later, that is in 1814, he was not given one automatically. The surveyors were directed to report whether any of Exmoor was suitable for growing oak timber, and a mere four years later they produced a report with the surprising opinion that large tracts could be planted with oak, ash, beech, birch, larch and fir, and the more reasonable recommendation that the Crown could well enclose and divide the Forest rather than renew the lease, selling some parts but keeping back others for timber.

In the next year, with Napoleon out of the way, the old oak forests were given a respite. But he who plants an acorn does so with an eye on the fifth and sixth generation of his children, and no one in 1815 foresaw ships of steel. An Act for inclosure was passed, and in two awards (1817 and 1819) the Inclosure Commissioners allotted approximately 10,000 acres to the king, 3,000 to Sir Thomas and 1,900 to Sir Charles Bamfylde, and parcels of land averaging thirty-one acres to the Free Suitors and Suitors at Large in meagre lieu of their grazing rights over an Exmoor a thousand times the size.

In the meantime, however, the Commissioners of Woods and Forests realized that it was impracticable to try to grow oak forests on Exmoor, and in 1818 they sold off the King's allotment by tender.

Seven tenders were received, ranging from Sir Thomas Acland's £5,000 to the £50,000 bid by John Knight of Worcestershire; and it was he and his family who, without previous knowledge of Exmoor or connection with it, would refashion and transform the face and economy of the ancient wilderness in the course of two generations.

The Knight family had prospered as ironmasters in Shropshire and Worcestershire ever since Cromwellian times, but they possessed the wide vision of the eighteenth century and its desire for improvement: mental, moral, physical and agricultural. John Knight's ancestor Richard Payne Knight, for example, had left a fine collection of classical bronzes, coins and gems to the British Museum. John, a disciple of Coke of Norfolk, was already farming in Worcestershire and had carried out land reclamation work there, and he saw in Exmoor the possibility not only of a successful venture but also of establishing in a former Royal Forest an estate extensive enough to match and support the wealth derived from iron; and though in the long run the Moor proved stubborn and readier to absorb his wealth than add to it, he persevered against odds, never wholly successful, but never defeated. In his expectations and his approach he may have been misinformed, but his spirit did not falter.

In his early days he met opposition, particularly from the Suitors at Large who, discontented with what seemed to them a paltry award of thirty-one acres, feared that Knight intended to take Brendon Common as well. His first constructional work was to build the Forest wall – twenty-nine miles of it – around the whole of his estate. Stretches of this survive today, especially from Black Barrow to Badgworthy and from Badgworthy towards Brendon

Pinkworthy Pond, within easy reach of Pinkworthy farm, but a haunt of silence and a strange place at twilight.

Old beech hedge with stone-faced bank, North Common.

Two Gates, as firm and well 'deeked' as in the years when it were made. Knight looked at the execrable roads, the packhorse tracks unfit for any wheeled traffic, and knew that until they were improved he could bring in no settlers, livestock or supplies and send nothing of consequence out. He therefore made up the tracks from Simonsbath, his 'capital', toward Exford and to Sandyway, built a good road to link up with the lowland road to South Molton, and an excellent carriageway from Simonsbath over the moor to Brendon and Lynmouth. Altogether twenty-two miles of road were made.

Installed in his new Great House at Simonsbath, John Knight engaged 200 Irish labourers and built a dam across the headwaters of the Barle west of the settlement to form a lake seven acres in extent and thirty feet deep at the northern end; Pinkworthy (or Pinkery) Pond. The reason is not known for sure, but a random remark suggests that he considered mining at Simonsbath and building a railway to take the ore to Porlock Weir, and the water from Pinkery would have been led along a 'canal' – which exists, but was badly surveyed – to work an incline, perhaps like the cliff railway built at Lynton in the 1890s.

John Knight, as a conscientious landlord, continued the ancient tradition of letting the grazing, but he was concerned to transform Exmoor from a waste into a prosperous community. He set to work to reclaim the land, digging many miles of ditch to drain off the water from the peaty surface, burning off the rough grass, liming the acid soil and deep-ploughing through the impermeable iron 'pan', and thus he created 2,500 acres of ploughland around Simonsbath.

His efforts, however, rarely brought the yield he was expecting, for the cold and heavy rainfall made the four-course rotation with wheat and barley, as he practised it in Worcestershire, impracticable here.

His stock-rearing experiments, on the other hand, were fairly successful. He brought in 700 head of cattle – West Highland bullocks and Herefords – and sizeable flocks of Cheviot sheep to add to the native Exmoor breed; but his experiments in crossing Exmoor mares with Arab stallions did not produce a pony robust enough to winter on the moor. But when in 1841 he handed over the management of Exmoor to his son Frederic, it was this partial success which pointed the way to consolidation.

Exmoor's often hostile climate caused problems for the Knights who aimed to transform the Moor from a waste to a prosperous community.

Well-maintained beech hedges lining the road, East Anstey Common.

Frederic saw that the Moor must be peopled and that farms and farming must be protected against a hostile climate. In place of his father's centralized work he built farms at Emmet's Grange, Driver, Duredon, Horsen, Larkbarrow, Pinkworthy, Tom's Hill, Warren and Wintershead and let them on favourable terms. He built scores of miles of beech hedges as windbreaks and worked out a system of root and grass growing so that the ewes could be folded down on these in the winter, ready for the spring lambing. He had limited family fortune but unlimited courage and resource; abandoning the hopeless attempt to grow cereals, he had found the true farming method, and although for many years most of his tenants, who came from away, failed for lack of experience, the Moor was in a fair way to becoming colonized. He built a school at Simonsbath and in 1856 added a church and parsonage and obtained the creation of a new 'Exmoor' parish. Between 1819 and 1857 the population of the Forest had risen from five to 281, and thirty children attended the village school.

From the mid-1860s Knight found tenants among local families. But as always, funds were short, and the shortage incited him to new enterprises with the

Cheviot sheep were brought to Exmoor by Frederic Knight in the 1870s.

hope of increasing income. In the 1850s he had gone into mining, with little success, but in the next decade, on the advice of his agent, Frederick Loveland Smyth, he began to reclaim more land by planting rape crops for three or four years in succession. The sheep throve on it and it helped decompose the soil down to below the 'pan'. At the end of that time the land, sown with a mixture of rape and grass seed, became permanent pasture – so permanent, indeed, that of the grassland that the Knights wrested from the Moor, virtually none has gone back.

Other experiments also met with success. The tenant at Wintershead in the early 1850s, Gerard Spooner, ran his holding as a Scottish sheep farm, with flocks of Cheviots and black-faced sheep, and brought down a shepherd, John Scott, who later became a stockman to Frederic Knight and also founded a farming dynasty on the Brendon Hills. Spooner's experiment failed – in Knight's opinion, because of 'the total ignorance of the surrounding people of the existence of any sheep except their own native breeds', of Exmoor Horn and Devon Closewool – but twenty years later Knight took it up with his customary vigour, brought in 5,000 Cheviots, a team of Scottish shepherds to tend them and established a flock which, even in the years of depression between the world wars, numbered 3,500 ewes, served by 100 rams.

By the mid-1870s and after half a century of trial, the Knights had found the way to farm Exmoor commercially, to enable knowledgeable farmers to gain a modest living from her without violating her nature. They arrived only just in time, for shortly afterwards Frederic Knight personally and the system he initiated and represented were struck devastating blows. His only son died, and this extinguished his hopes of founding a landed dynasty; and in 1878 and 1879 the combination of phenomenally wet summers and the first shipments of grain from the vast prairies of North America and of refrigerated meat from Australia and New Zealand drove both cereal and stock farming into a depression which lasted until the Second World War. The Exmoor farmers weathered the storms better than most, perhaps because their way of life had engendered hardihood, self-reliance, thrift and moderate expectations; and certainly because their sheep were bred mainly for wool and their cattle rearing never went beyond the dimensions that the local markets could absorb.

When Sir Frederic, knighted for his public services, died in 1897, he was still farming about 9,000 acres with a stock of some 9,000 ewes and lambs and maintaining 'his interest in what had been the biggest task of a very busy life right up to the end.'

'His disappointments had been many, his reverses severe, but it would be impossible to find an example, in the length and breadth of England, of courage, determination and resource greater than that which he had displayed in his effort to complete the stupendous task conceived and started by his father, of the reclamation of Exmoor Forest.'

6 **The Moor after the Knights**

Exmoor, by and large, remained for forty years as Sir Frederic Knight had left it, except that in the 1920s and 1930s some of the roads were widened and improved, notably those from Winsford to Exford and on to Simonsbath and from Simonsbath to Brendon and Lynton. Many of the farmers acquired cars, if usually second-hand ones, and the day-long drives to and from Barnstaple or South Molton markets contracted to an hour. The summers brought day-trippers in 'charabancs', with little advantage to the people of the Moor; but more welcome were the visitors who came for a week or two, occupied all the spare accommodation, found its simplicity more than compensated for by the generous hospitality, and feasted, antedating their personal Elysiums, on 'urts' (whortleberries) and Exmoor clotted cream. 'This summer harvest,' observed CS Orwin 'plays an important part in the farming economy of the district'.

With 1939 Exmoor was brought into violent contact with the modern world. For the first time in perhaps 2,000 years she suffered the physical ravages of war. She saw no hostile troops, of course, other than prisoner-of-war farm workers and the German airman who baled out from his stricken Dornier and tried to surrender to a farm worker Home Guard, only to be told 'I can't be bothered wi' thee now, I be late fer work as 'tis'. The legends of an Anson training 'plane sunk in the depths of Pinkworthy Pond and an American tank buried deep in a bog on The Chains are still waiting to be disproved; but Larkbarrow and Tom's Hill were used as training grounds, and gunnery reduced the farmhouses to ruins. Thus does war, even in defence, bring desolation and darkness to places remote from the scenes of its raging.

Other changes came more insidiously, prompted by the needs of the nation, benefiting a few but modifying again the nature of the Moor. In July 1939 Parliament, belatedly sensing that the milennium of peace might be postponed for a while, brought in ploughing grants, followed by special subsidies for hill ewes in 1941 and for hill cattle in 1943. The

This beech hedge has been broken and worn away by the passage of cattle.

resultant changes were most noticeable on the Honeymead estate, where the owner was able to make a large capital investment, sometimes without regard to the short-term economies.

By the end of the war 1,175 acres had been ploughed and reclaimed, carrying nearly 2,500 sheep and 150 cattle. The neglect of seventy years had been made good, and Exmoor, thanks to the deep ploughing and generous dressings of stone-dust lime and triple phosphate, was producing more food than ever before.

The pace slackened for a while as the tension of wartime eased, but in 1952 Exmoor, which in the minds of most people elsewhere had figured as no more than a holiday destination for eccentric lovers of solitude, came into the national consciousness with shocking effect. July was a wet month, and for the first fortnight of August it rained almost incessantly, so that the ground all over the moor became saturated. In the high region of The Chains it could take no more. On this morass, in the twenty-four hours of the fifteenth of August, there fell a terrifying eight inches of rain, and round Longstone Barrow nine inches; and this mountain of water, over half-a-million tons of it from every square mile,

streamed off the moor by every channel, goyal and combe. Every runnel became a torrent and every torrent a raging flood. The River Barle uprooted trees, bore them irresistibly along, battered the bridge at Landacre, tore away the ten-ton stones of Tarr Steps and flooded Simonsbath to a depth of ten feet; but in the north the damage was catastrophic and awesome. The north-west moor drains into the narrow, steep-sided valleys – or rather, gorges – of the East and West Lyn, and on that dreadful night the flood of water, unable to spread laterally, built up into a tremendous wall, tore boulders from their beds – someone has calculated 100,000 tons – and bore them onward and downward, falling upon the villages of Barbrook and Lynmouth and sweeping away cottages, churches, bridges, roads and more than thirty human lives.

But the flood, though catastrophic for certain communities, and later floods in 1960, only briefly interrupted the evolution of the moorland economy. From about 1950 this began to accelerate, and when Exmoor was designated a national park in 1954 the threat to the open moorland could be clearly seen. For fifteen years national agricultural policies, as administered by successive governments of

The fine medieval bridge at Landacre (pronounced Lannaker) carrying the road from Exford to North Molton; first recorded in 1610.

different complexions, had encouraged farmers to produce food heedless of concern for protecting the beauty of the landscape. The Ministry of Agriculture and the Ministry of Works and Local Government, the forerunner of the Department of the Environment, worked at loggerheaded cross-purposes, the first encouraging and subsidising the farming community to plough the unreclaimed moor, the second tacitly opposing this policy but lacking the funds and, some suspected, the will to make opposition effective. In other words, the clients of one government department were encouraged to despoil the beauty that another department, eventually the Exmoor National Park Authority, was constituted to protect.

Rather than enumerate the scores of examples of moorland lost to the nation, however, one episode in one particular area may be taken as an emblem of the struggle between developers – though this time not agricultural – and conservers from 1950 onward: the threat to The Chains posed in the spring of 1958 by the Forestry Commission's plans for them, a threat only warded off by concerted and dedicated action by a small number of people enlisting the support of many.

The Chains, mentioned earlier in connection with the floods of 1952, form the largest tract of fairly level ground on Exmoor, extending from Somerset into Devon and ranging in height from just under 1,500 to 1,600 feet. The annual rainfall is sixty to seventy inches, and even when it is not raining the atmosphere is moist. They have had, and still have, a fearsome reputation as a home of mist-borne dangers – 'notoriously misty and boggy', according to a modern archaeologist, and a Master of Hounds who was also an MP observed, 'I would sooner be anywhere on Exmoor, *except on The Chains*, in the thickest fog, than in the House of Commons.' Four rivers, the Exe, Barle, West Lyn and Hoaroak Water, take their rise here. The 'iron pan' makes the surface soil waterlogged, the soil water is acid and the ground windswept by all seasons. In short, it is as inhospitable a place, and as attractive to lovers of solitude, as may be found almost anywhere in southern England.

A 'blanket bog' has developed, one of the very few in the west of England where the dominant plant is the deer sedge, and this and the relative scarcity of other plants – very little ling, no bell heather and a mere handful of varieties of fern, grasses and other sedge – have combined to provide naturalists

Tarr Steps, over the River Barle, the longest clapper bridge in England but of unknown age. More than once it has been damaged or swept away by flood but rebuilt, most recently by Royal Engineers in 1961.

Lynmouth rebuilt, with the river bed straightened and deepened, after the disastrous floods of 1952.

with a field of interest and enquiry; comparisons with the results of grazing and peat digging practice elsewhere suggest that the vegetation here has not basically changed for a thousand years. But aesthetic considerations were seen as hardly less important. Here was one of the highest and most visible expanses of the whole Moor, and it would be covered with row upon marching row of sombre conifers. When the plans of the Forestry Commission became known, a small action group in north Devon launched an Exmoor Preservation Petition and collected 3,000 signatures to support the Exmoor National Park Authority's opposition to the scheme. At length the Forestry Commission backed down and The Chains were saved. As a direct result the Exmoor Society was formed in the autumn of the same year. It flourishes still with over a thousand members and a history of active support for conservation and land purchase. It has commissioned an exhaustive land survey and authoritative reports on controversial questions, and generally acted as provocative gadfly to those it sees, rightly or wrongly, as somnolent guardians of the public cause.

The saving of The Chains from afforestation,

however, must be set against a background of long-continuing loss of moorland to 'improvement' for profit. Exmoor assumed a new national importance focusing attention on such improvement of marginal lands (as were the Norfolk Broads and Somerset Levels). In the mid-1960s the loss was running at 1,000 acres a year and some observers feared that Exmoor, as a wild place, might disappear completely by the end of the century. In 1965 the Exmoor Society commissioned the rising young landscape consultant Geoffrey Sinclair to undertake a botanical survey of the entire park, and his study formed the basis of a historic pamphlet, *Can Exmoor Survive?*, issued in time for the National Parks Conference at Lynton the following year. This aroused strong opposition among the farming and landowning interests, but by this time the National Park Authority was also coming round to the conservation cause. It defined sensitive areas as being of 'critical amenity' value and introduced a voluntary notification scheme to encourage farmers to consult before undertaking 'improvements' and see if some accommodation could be reached. But it also warned the Government that unless it were given greater powers and resources it could not protect the moorland.

In 1968 the Government brought in a Countryside Act, but this had more to do with access and recreation in lowland England and Wales and had little effect on the national parks. The attrition went on, and public pressure built up, until nine years later, in response to it, the Government commissioned Lord Porchester to conduct an enquiry into the reclamation of moorland for improved grazing. The report that emerged gave hope and direction for the first time, that the further loss of this national asset, the open unspoilt moorland, might be averted or at least contained.

The report confirmed that 12,000 acres – nearly twenty square miles, or one-tenth of Exmoor – had been converted to farming or forestry in the thirty years since 1946. The National Park Authority acted. It prepared two maps – precursors, incidentally, to the Section 43 maps required in the Wildlife and Countryside Act of 1981. The first defined all areas of the park predominantly moor or heath, the second defined tracts within these which ought for their beauty or scientific interest to be conserved in their semi-natural state for ever. But the national parks are not the property of the nation. Exmoor is owned by a host of individuals and institutions, and the Authority could not ignore, even if it had wished to, the age-old presumption that a farmer is the best and only judge of the most profitable and fitting use to make of his land and must not be interfered with except in dire emergency. The strength and tenacity with which this belief was held cannot be overstated, and the Authority undertook to enter into a management agreement with any farmer seeking to reclaim or 'improve' such land within the Map One area for which the Ministry of Agriculture would normally have paid him a subsidy. In return for his restraint – which did not mean leaving the land to revert to a wild state but keeping it in good heart by grazing with sheep and cattle – and for renouncing the profit that reclamation would have given him, the Authority would compensate him on guidelines agreed with the Countryside Commission, Country Landowners' Association and National Farmers' Union. To achieve this agreement cost the officers of the Authority eighteen months of patient and sometimes frustrating negotiation, and in one respect their hopes were disappointed.

Lord Porchester had also recommended that if persuasion and the pendent carrot failed, the National Park Authority should have power to invoke a Moorland Conservation Order which would either serve its obvious purpose or safeguard access, or both combined. This sanguine hope did not survive the change of government in 1979, and when the provision struggled through to the 1981 Countryside Act, the management agreements had been relegated to a merely voluntary status.

Meanwhile, however, very largely thanks to the Authority's persuasion, the atmosphere had improved and the arguments had become less strident. Many farmers had come to realize that conservation stood for more than an urbanites' ploy and had accepted the need of restraint for posterity's sake. Conservers, for their part, had acknowledged that if a farmer were barred from farming as he saw fit, he had a legitimate grievance. They accepted the environmental half-loaf of voluntary management agreements and the farming community as a whole accepted that they could live within restraints if they were decently compensated for it.

The system worked, up to a point; but if a farmer wanted to plough and forfeit compensation, the Authority could delay him for a time. The taxpayer continued to pay the penalty for a muddle of policies

Warren Farm has been bought by the National Park Authority and is run as a working farm with an element of experiment.

which encouraged the farmer to produce more each year and then compensated him for not producing it.

Eventually, in 1985, the accumulation of food surpluses in Europe made the European Community reconsider its subsidy policy. Grants ceased to be payable for deep ploughing and converting moorland, and the conservers breathed more freely when the Ministry of Agriculture, Fisheries and Food announced grants for maintaining hedges and drystone walls. But even these measures did not safeguard the Moor completely. In the same year a farmer proposed to plough 440 acres of grazing land at Long Holcombe and grow cereals. At 1,400 feet above sea level with a rainfall of 60 inches? The idea might seem laughable, but the Park Authority had to take it seriously. Whether laughable or not, it had MAFF backing! A management agreement was refused by the owner, and the Authority then saw no choice but to capitulate and pay £180,000 to buy and safeguard 440 acres of land which, many believed, would never have grown cereals economically and might not have been at risk if the ransom money had not been available. Will this, they wonder, set a new and destructive pattern for the Moor? Or will the Government step in, even if belatedly, and enact legislation to prevent the exploiting of a great but wasting national asset for private gain? Against experience, they continue to hope.

7 **Buildings of Exmoor**

In the first pages of this book there appeared a geological map of Exmoor, looking for all the world like a first study for a Daliesque portrait of a recumbent headless zebra. One of the attractions of the district is its variety of native architecture – gladly ignoring as far as possible the more recent imported abominations – and that variety stems directly from the geology. Up till recent times the roads were poor, merchandise was transported by packhorse, and carts were virtually unknown; so a landowner or farmer wishing to build a house took the material closest to hand. This had two effects, the one intentional, the other consequential: he built cheaply, but his building matched its surroundings, and besides this, inheriting and working within a vernacular style of building which had been tested by the sensibility of many generations, he built with

'He built with an eye for the fitness of things' – Chidgley Farm in Old Cleeve parish, north eastern slopes of the Brendon Hills

Drystone wall, near
Simonsbath.

an eye for the fitness of things.

Looking about you, then, as you travel the Moor you will find in each neighbourhood the geology and, to some extent, the weather reflected in the style of the native buildings, and you will be struck by the diversity of colour imparted by the sedimentary Devonian rocks – from pink to deep reddish purple, from fawn to rust and dark brown, from light grey to near black. The proportions vary from one locality to another: Lynton, for example, is largely a grey and brown town, but the buildings of Minehead, particularly those of the late nineteenth and early twentieth centuries, seem more consistently red than elsewhere.

The pleasant and workable rich red rocks, however, lie deep under the Moor and only approach the surface on the eastern edge, yet you will see Exmoor at its most typical not in that part, but in the old farms of the higher moor. As in every other upland area, the farmhouses, outbuildings and walls were all built of local natural materials, used in the way that suited them best; but if you also know Dartmoor, you will straightway recognize here a different style. All Exmoor stone, of any colour, is difficult to cut and work. Unlike the granite boulders of a Dartmoor farm, the 'rag', compacted shillet, breaks away in unshapely masses, and consequently walls are made of uncoursed rubble work – and to an Exmoor eye they are none the less attractive for that. The buildings tend to be long, low, plain and severe. They were no larger than was needed and were often built right against the hillsides, seeming to merge into the landscape.

The old builders were realists. They built their

farms as fortresses to withstand a hostile climate and
set them in hollows sheltered from the winter gales,
tight groups of stone buildings weathered grey, and
backed by wind-breaks of beech trees. Openings
faced on to the yards which the buildings enclosed,
the house on one side, the barns and shippons on
the others, presenting blank walls to the outside.
Search Exmoor as you may, you will be hard put to it
to find a farm standing exposed on a wind-swept
hill.

All building on the high moor speaks of the
challenge of the weather: the walls two or three feet
thick; the massive chimney breasts; the wide, deep
porches sheltering the doorways; the windows
small, square-paned and widely spaced; the
medium-pitched, short-spanned roofs which
overhang by a handsbreadth, covered with stone
tiles or very occasionally thatched; the outer walls
plain, workaday and unadorned or, when facing the
weather, hung with local slate. Out on the land, the
field walls show the same simplicity, their stones
laid row on uneven row and capped with flat stones
set on end; while the great hedgebanks such as
those bounding the Forest are faced or 'deeked'

A farm building,
Simonsbath.

with flat stones set edgewise and vertically into them.

Underfoot, the courts of the farms are paved with the same stone broken fairly small and rolled in, though near the coast pebbles are made to serve.

Cottages on Selworthy Green, built by Sir Thomas Acland for estate workers and pensioners in the mid-nineteenth century.

So much for the high moor. Descending into the sheltered combes you will find the architecture recognizably the same but subtly changed. The roofs no longer overhang to the same extent, dormer windows project above the eaves and guttering is fixed to the walls, Thatch is more common, and in the Vale of Porlock round chimneys and external bread ovens add a characteristic touch rarely found elsewhere, a softness repeated in the architecture of the barns, with their heavy thatched roofs supported on slender timber uprights or rounded pillars.

Both on the upland and in the vale, however, the old farmhouses have a design which recalls a primitive age: a long passage runs from front to back of the building, with doors opening off. When built on a sloping site, the higher part formed the living quarters, the lower a winter shelter for the beasts.

The red sandstone, as mentioned earlier, is not commonly seen in houses or cottages except in the neighbourhood of the coastal plain near Minehead and Porlock. When it is used, it combines dignity with warmth, but even here the more usual materials are rubble stone and – very occasionally – cob, a mixture of pounded clay and straw good for centuries when well protected. Both stone and cob are usually covered with a coat of rough-cast and washed white or cream. (The deplorable suburban

Nettlecombe Court, a Jacobean rebuilding of a manor house with a fourteenth century church, in the red sandstone country.

pink is a recent innovation.) You may regret this concealment, but sadly the warm red sandstone, no matter how pleasing to the eye, weathers badly and after fifty or sixty years' exposure becomes saturated and almost porous, and rough-cast compensates for its deficiency. The few great houses in red sandstone, by reason of their status and social function, show little that is peculiar to Exmoor. They are built in a national style, whether Elizabethan, Jacobean or Victorian. Nevertheless, having seen Dunster Castle, Combe Sydenham or Nettlecombe Court, you will not soon forget them.

No less characteristic than the dwellings of Exmoor are its churches, speaking as they do of a region where the scarcity of a reluctant soil was conquered by tenacious hardihood. Something of that, it seems to me, is to be read in the squat, square grey towers of Culbone, Oare and Stoke Pero (the 'parishes three where no passun 'll go'), in Countisbury and the Brendon churches of Cutcombe, Brompton Ralph, Clatworthy and Withiel Florey, though a white rendering has softened the sternness of the last-named. Perhaps the plainest of all, and among the most cherished, is the rough-cast, lime-washed church of Rodhuish; a simple, undivided structure with small early English windows, crowned with a pyramidal roof surmounted by a cone and weathervane.

Such roof-crowned towers add a delightful touch to several Exmoor churches. Treborough has a similar pyramid, roofed with slates from the quarry a mere slate's throw away; Timberscombe, a hexagonal roof; Porlock, an octagonal one,

An old painting of Dunster showing the yarn market.

curiously truncated, (and this church is also worth visiting for the fourteenth-century Harington effigies, which, though of Derbyshire and not Exmoor origin, have been ranked among the first in the county). Luxborough and Wootton Courtenay towers have saddleback roofs added by Victorian restorers.

But whenever medieval Exmoor man found himself in more favourable surroundings and 'felt the soul within him climb', his imagination – or his ambition – took wings and he built churches more commodious and not a little elegant, as at Selworthy, Luccombe, Timberscombe, Nettlecombe or Winsford; and in later days, as at Molland, Exford, Selworthy or Kingsbrompton, he adorned them within and without. If, then, you wish to see local church-building and decoration at their richest,

Withiel Florey church.

most graceful and most highly developed, be sure at least to visit Selworthy, Timberscombe, Exford and, of course, Dunster. But for Exmoor at its most typical, simple, unadorned, unimproved and still virtually unspoilt, then to Culbone, Oare, Trentishoe and Withycombe you should go.

Then see the chapels, particularly the simple structures dating from the early and mid-nineteenth century, before the Gothic revival had spread to the district. They were mostly built by or for Bible Christian or Wesleyan congregations of farmers, labourers and tradesmen on whatever few constricted wayside sites could be had. These simple buildings present to the casual glance, as Lewis H Court remarks 'bare walls and their windows staringly plain'; but gradually the eye – the

Timberscombe church, in the Vale of Avill.

inward eye, maybe – perceives their humble dignity and their rightness for the untutored but thoughtful men and women who filled them a century and more ago. Few of them still serve their first purpose, and the forms and outlines of others lie concealed within the dwelling-places to which they have been adapted, as at Exford, Bury, Luckwell Bridge, Winsford, Bridgetown, Withypool and Gupworthy. The shapely windows of Kingsbrompton and Timberscombe chapels – the former grimly slate-hung but inwardly elegant – bear witness to the refinement of the Burston and Cording families who founded and built them in the 1830s and 1850s, and the style of Beulah on Brendon Hill, uncharacteristic of Exmoor, recalls the Cornish miners who worked here in the quarter century between 1853 and 1878. Withypool is described by Sir Nikolaus Pevsner, never an over-indulgent critic, as 'very pretty with Gothic ogee-headed doorway and windows'. Of the later, neo-Gothic chapels, Upton, on the southern edge of the national park, is built on two levels, with a basement stable for the preacher's horse, while Roadwater, in the north east, is an imposing red sandstone building in Early English style and of historical interest as the

Roadwater, a close-knit village sheltered from the prevailing winds in a valley running north from the Brendon Hills.

last Bible Christian chapel to be built (in 1907) in England. It also houses a singularly sweet-toned organ.

I have written so far of our traditional buildings, formed of native material and shaped by centuries of tested tradition. But if the older Exmoor villages were, so to speak, an architectural Eden, of recent years the serpent has performed assiduously. In Dulverton, Roadwater and Porlock you may see 'developments' which would cause no remark in suburbia and would win a star of merit from Whitehall but are utterly at variance with the native style. Those who built our villages placed their cottages in a more than admired disorder, an ideal disorder, which best employed the limited space of the river valleys, and which placed a man within an arm's length of his neighbour but still gave him seclusion and privacy. The modern developer, urged by the planner, squanders space as if it were time, and places his victims in sight of one another like exhibits at a raree-show. Old Exmoor built its cottages by the roadside and left its lanes unspoilt. The developer sweeps away the ancient hedges and creates an asphalt wilderness; and in place of the infinitely variegated Devonian rock, the 'rag',

Rose Cottage, Dulverton, a traditional building in keeping with its surroundings.

sandstone and slate, he uses reconstituted stone, an amalgam of compressed dust which has the polychromatic finesse of a pillar-box and after decades of weathering still remains drab but incorrigible. And here and there, as at Wheddon Cross, you may see houses with blank walls like insults and pointed gable ends flung up like defiant javelins. How did such lamentable structures, such memorials to ugliness and greed, pass the planner, you may wonder – but there are laws of libel, and I will not be drawn. Like the poet in Dante, let us not speak of them, but look, and pass by.

Bury Bridge, and the hamlet of Bury are well worth the detour from the Exe valley road, but the bridge should not be driven over!

8 **Exmoor at work**

Few areas of England wholly escaped the ravages of the Industrial Revolution and the population explosion of the nineteenth century, but Exmoor almost did, and the visible wounds inflicted on the landscape eventually healed.

By good fortune, as it turned out, Exmoor had poor communications and lacked the resources that the new industrialists would pounce on. Roads, nil; navigable rivers, nil; canals, nil, and no reasonable prospect of constructing any; harbours, three, but small, serving local trade, and situated on a rocky, hostile coast with dangerous currents offshore; coal, nil; iron ore, some, but no one realized it; other minerals, likewise. So Exmoor escaped.

Yet seen from another point of view, she was already bearably industrialized when the nineteenth century began, and because her industry depended on indigenous talent and more traditional sources of power than the mills or factories of Lancashire and Yorkshire, it perhaps affords greater interest today than a more spectacular intervention and development from outside would have done. Exmoor was in fact a region of small, local industries, each serving little more than one village and the immediate neighbourhood and innocent of offence because it

Even today small industries are being established on Exmoor. Here, New Mills, Luxborough, where the West Somerset Small Industries Group was set up in 1977.

Dunster Mill, showing
twin overshot wheels.

took energy not from polluting fossil fuels but from
falling water.

The total of water mills worked by the dozens of
streams and waters radiating from the heart of
Exmoor has never been calculated exactly, but it
must have numbered at least fifty, to judge from the
little stream, nameless except to geographers,
which rises on the northern slopes of the Brendon
Hills near Luxborough and Treborough and flows
down converging valleys to Roadwater and thence,
as one river, to the sea. Its combined lengths come
to no more than twelve miles, but in industry's
heyday – almost up to within living memory – it
drove fifteen mills, including grist, fulling, blade,
paper and saw mills. Most of the machinery has
gone, but the buildings still stand, and if the leats
serving them were cleared and repaired the old

mills could sing at their work again. (One of them, at Dunster, has been restored in the past few years; it now grinds corn as a working mill and is open to the public; but a large scale Ordnance Survey map will lead you to the sites of many more.)

The multifarious mills served an industrial evolution rather than revolution, providing the power for many activities besides those mentioned above, such as the agricultural machinery firms of John and James Brayley of Molland and the mechanical farm work of the Norman family at Gupworthy Farm only a few feet below the highest level of the Brendon Hills. The village of Roadwater, in a north-eastern valley, showed an astonishing variety: two grist mills, a fulling mill, a blade mill, a foundry and agricultural engineering works, all powered by water.

Every human institution from empire to hamlet enjoys its hour of perfection before it either declines or is transmuted to serve some new purpose. For the Exmoor village – leaving out of account the social injustice and endemic poverty – that hour, that age rather, lasted an indeterminate length of time in the nineteenth century and began to fade in the 1880s; but up to then the village led a self-contained and virtually self-sufficient life. To cite the village last named, with its 500 inhabitants in the 1870s and 1880s it enjoyed, with the mills already mentioned, the services of a baker, butcher, grocer, chandler, two shoe-makers and cordwainers, a cobbler, tailor, two smiths, a post office, saddler and harnessmaker, wheelwright, carpenter, two masons, photographer, music teacher, minister and chapel, railway station, assembly hall and three inns. A mile away a slate quarry provided work for thirty men, and the surrounding countryside was dotted with sawpits, charcoal burners' sites and lime kilns to produce dressing for the upland fields. Most of these activities persisted in diminished form into the 1920s and 1930s, until the cumulative effects of a world war, mechanization, rural depression, depopulation and cheap public transport ended the old village life.

All this industry, however, as remarked earlier, was local in conception and served local needs, in contrast to the classic industrial development. Only in one field did the latter involve Exmoor and leave visible trace: mining.

Exmoor's chief ore has been iron, with here and there, in small quantities, manganese, copper, zinc

Silver-mine building on Knap Down, near Combe Martin.

and antimony, and most of the activity was crowded into the second half of the nineteenth century. On the western fringes of Exmoor, however, the story goes back many generations, and Daniel Defoe, touring Devon and Somerset in the 1720s, reported, 'About Ilfracomb, Comb Mertin, also at Delverton, . . . they have been at work to see if they can recover some silver mines, which in the reign of King Edward III were so large that they employed three hundred miners, and brought that prince great sums of money for the carrying on his wars against France: What progress they are now like to make in it, I cannot yet learn' – but they did, even though intermittently, and mined silver and lead until the 1880s. One old working reputedly runs under the main street of Combe Martin (which lies just outside the national park), and as recently as 1983 some cottages being renovated were judged to be in danger of collapse. Yet nothing visible remains of six centuries' venture but a gaunt ruin on a hill (SS 587467).

Of the iron ore workings, on the other hand, a great deal of evidence remains, and some still wait to be explored.

A nebulous tradition had it that the 'Romans' – though popular lore sometimes confused them with the Roman Catholics! – dug for iron ore on Exmoor, but the discovery of implements from Roman days and spoil heaps of an ancient date hardly constitute proof. One Michael Wynston obtained a licence to dig for iron ore in 1550, and German miners were thought to have worked here, as they did in Cumberland, in the reign of Queen Elizabeth – whence the name Eisen or Iron Hill (SS 904371). Leaving aside these rumours, iron ore was certainly being mined in the 1830s and 1840s on the estate of Sir John Lethbridge at Chargot, Luxborough (SS 977357). This was small-scale work, but when a sample of the haematite ore was put on show at the Great Exhibition of 1851, the iron content of sixty per cent caused a Welsh ironmaster, Ebenezer Rogers, to raise his entrepreneurial eyebrows. He formed a syndicate, which brought Cornish, Welsh and North Country miners to West Somerset, and between 1853 and 1878 the men of the Brendon Hills Iron Ore Company sank or drove no fewer than thirty-one shafts and adits and brought out three-quarters of a million tons of iron ore, reaching their peak for a year's production with 46,894 tons in 1877. Miners' cottages and chapels were built at Brendon Hill and Gupworthy, and stores, pumping houses, winding gear housings, engine sheds and an aerial ropeway rose above the beech hedges. But in 1878 high-grade ore from Spain was imported at a price the Brendon Hill mines could not compete with. At their peak they had employed 300 men, now they closed down as if overnight. The miners and their families departed, their homes at Gupworthy became a ghost village, the workings filled with 150 million gallons of water, and the rain and the wind undid the fabric that remained.

But that is only part of the story, and the more transient part, for the enterprise left other traces which can be seen today.

The iron ore for smelting had to be transported from Brendon Hill down to the port of Watchet and shipped thence to Barry in South Wales. In the first year of the mining it became clear that horses and carts could never cope with the tonnage. The company must have a railway. But here was the problem. The mine heads were within sight of the sea but 1,200 feet above it, and no steam locomotive could negotiate the equivalent of a one in twenty-six gradient for eight miles – which in any case was an engineering impossibility in this countryside. But these Victorians, seeing problems rather as opportunities, had their answer. They brought their mineral line up the river valley for six miles at a gentle uniform gradient of one in 100 to the foot of the great escarpment of the Brendon Hills. From

A mine building at Burrow Farm, Brendon Hill. Plans are afoot to restore this and create an interpretation centre for the former iron-ore mines and mineral railway.

there they blasted and dug and shovelled their way up to the top in a stupendous mile-long one-in-four incline which still today compels admiration and sets the imagination racing. 'You could lay golden sovereigns side by side all the way up for what it cost them,' my father used to say – and at £50,000 of real money he was scarcely exaggerating.

The incline was 'worked' on a simple principle. A truck at the top, filled with iron ore, was attached by a steel cable which went round an upright drum eighteen feet in diameter, to an empty truck at the foot of the incline. The full truck, released from the top, pulled up the empty one with the three-and-a-half ton length of cable, and the constantly varying ratios of weight were controlled by a winding engine and brake gear.

From here the mineral line was taken across the main road and continued west along the top of the hills, past mine heads, engine houses, spoil tips, on embankments and through cuttings, for another four miles to the terminus near Gupworthy. Most of its length can be traced without difficulty, and plans are afoot to restore and interpret the best preserved of these remains. But in the meantime, if you mean to visit them, may I suggest you always seek the permission of the farmer before you do. He is not a difficult man to find.

The mines and their railway have left a profound impression on the consciousness of the native people of the seaward slopes of the Brendon Hills. Sayings of long-dead railwaymen still form part of everyday speech; and the Raleigh's Cross Inn and many households treasure photographs of the

Installing the 18 inch drums in the winding house at the top of Brendon Hill Incline in 1858. (From a conception of Michael H Jones.)

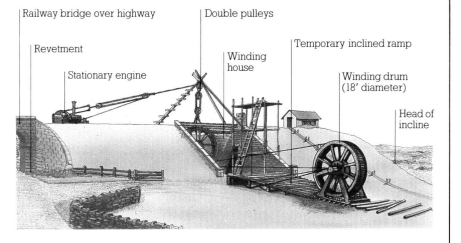

Railway bridge over highway | Double pulleys

Revetment

Stationary engine

Winding house

Temporary inclined ramp

Winding drum (18' diameter)

Head of incline

The mineral line, west of
Brendon Hill Farm.

different aspects of the 'Mineral Line'. Plans for the
conservation of the remaining structures arouse
intense interest, though performance waits as ever
on funds. Of all the opening gambits that you, as a
visitor to the north east of the district, can employ,
'What can you tell me about the Mineral Line?' is the
most likely to bring the feast of reason – and
sometimes unreason – and flow of soul that you hope
for.

Other mines, at the far end of the Moor, produced
a greater variety of ore and for longer than those of
Brendon Hill. Those fifteenth-century German
miners may have come first on the scene, but the
Bampfylde or Poltimore Mines near Heasley Mill
were worked sporadically in the seventeenth and
eighteenth centuries and attained their chief
development between 1870 and 1890. They mainly
produced copper, but also some iron ore, silver
and a little gold (mostly in the iron). In these later
years also the Florence Mine, near Tabor Hill,
yielded a large quantity of spathic iron ore suitable
for steel-making by the Bessemer process. The ores
were taken to the outside world by a narrow-gauge
tramway built in 1874 to connect with the main line of
the Devon and Somerset Railway a little to the east of

Heasley Mill, near North Molton; the head of the 800 foot shaft.

South Molton station; in the fields below Marsh Farm the banking can still be seen.

Taking the whole of the Exmoor area, no fewer than sixty mines have been exploited or at least prospected at one time or another, but working in the heart of the Moor met with scant success and disappointed the expectations of Frederic Knight; but the marks the mines left on the Barle Valley near Simonsbath can be seen today, and as their story forms a monument to Victorian tenacity they should not be passed over.

Cornham is a mineral-bearing area, and at Cornham Ford an adit runs into the hillside for nearly half a mile; but the very le: gth of the adit and the depth of shafts elsewhere indicate that the ore was hard to get at and the yield uneconomic. The nearby Wheal Eliza mine promised a rich haul but produced a decade of frustration; however the knowledge that it contained copper and manganese as well as iron sufficed to persuade normally hard-headed mining engineers between 1845 and 1857 to drive an adit, sink a shaft 300 feet deep, install a five-foot water-wheel and work doggedly for small returns despite flood, drought and a chronic shortage of funds. After almost ten years they struck ore analysing up to sixty per cent metallic iron, and Frederic Knight, anticipating a source of income for his agricultural experiments, bought the lease and negotiated with the Dowlais Iron Company to provide the iron-work for a railway to the coast at Porlock Weir. The incline at Brendon Hill had shown how the problems of altitude and gradient could be overcome; and if that was impressive, Knight's creation would – considering the time and the resources – have been magnificent. But all too soon the partners fell out. The yield of iron ore was disappointing, and Frederic Knight contended that he had never disguised his inability to construct the railway at his own expense. The Company retorted that the railway was no use to them without payable ore to be transported. The project fell through.

Something, however, remained, and if you persist you will find here and there lengths of the railway alignment which were dug but never metalled – for after his initial enthusiasm Knight's work on the line seems to have been perfunctory. Still, the traces which remain give sufficient idea of a plan which, if carried through, would have created one of the engineering wonders of the 1850s.

So Wheal Eliza will repay anyone's visit, not least for the substantial work of restoration and presentation carried out there by the Park Authority in recent years. As an added attraction there also clings to Wheal Eliza the aura of a gruesome, 'foul and most unnatural murder' committed by one William Burgess in 1858 on his little daughter Anna; and if that does not entice the visitor, then the burgeoning tourist industry of Exmoor has no real hope.

But of course it has, and while we should hesitate to identify tourism as the economic salvation of the Western world, it is the main industry to which Exmoor will be looking to diversify its economy and

Artist's impression of Wheal Eliza mine in its working days.

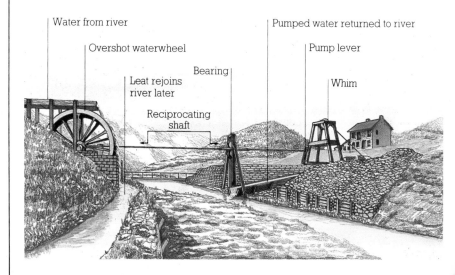

Water from river

Pumped water returned to river

Overshot waterwheel

Pump lever

Bearing

Whim

Leat rejoins river later

Reciprocating shaft

Thatching a cottage, Selworthy Green. This ancient craft is enjoying a happy revival and providing employment for skilled people.

fill the void caused by the changed conditions of agriculture. Other new and revived crafts and industries on a human and acceptable scale have sprung up in the villages – boatbuilding, light engineering, furniture making, pottery, gold and silver plating, trout farming, wrought iron work, textile manufacture, forestry, glassblowing, scientific instrument manufacture, sawmills, woodcraft – but it would be idle to list the details of a frequently changing and kaleidoscopic scene. However, it is worth remarking that in 1977 the Exmoor National Park, at New Mills, Luxborough, saw the birth of a West Somerset Small Industries Group which has since expanded to serve the whole county of Somerset with outstanding success and can be taken as a model for the encouragement of commercial and industrial initiative and enterprise.

9 **Legend and tradition**

The lonely places of Exmoor, the solitary trackways and wooded combes, the forbidding, tussocky 'zogs' and morasses where no birds sing, the roll and sweep of heathland leading the eye to a blue distance where earth, sea and sky imperceptibly merge, all these make for mystery, and mystery creates legend.

A rigorous historian may look askance at legend as unprovable, but seen in a more positive way as the oral tradition of a pre-literate society, it gives evidence of experiences and happenings for which the historian will never find documentary proof.

Exmoor holds a store of ancient mysteries and capriciously – if rarely – makes them visible to one person and not to another. To be paranormally sensitive to the unseen does not guarantee a glimpse, but nor does complete disbelief form a

Ice on hedgerows, near Five Barrows.

barrier; and no matter how rare and unpredictable the visions, anyone walking – especially *walking* – over Exmoor may, at any moment, sense an unaccountable strangeness and unseen presence. Such a moment is as likely to come in the heat and glare of a noon in high summer as at dusk in an autumn mist; but there is little to fear on Exmoor, and so the thrill of the uncanny moment is pleasant rather than not.

East Lyn gorge from
county gate.

All the same, figures from the unknown past have
apparently been dimly imprinted as if on the air
itself, and since no rational explanation carries
conviction, you may prefer an irrational one; and
some of these imprints reputedly persist as if time
had lost all dominion over them. At a certain
barrow, for instance, its guardian spirit is said to
have been seen, a huge indeterminate but human
form covered in matted hair; at another barrow
your horse may shy and refuse to pass for abject
fear; and, as recorded elsewhere, the Exmoor
writer S H Burton, walking on the ancient trackway of
the harepath found himself alongside a company of
travellers from some far-off age. One family has
claimed three generations' acquaintance with that
diminutive people the 'piskies'.

Traditions have a life of their own and cling
tenaciously to localities for even a thousand years
after those who created them: at Dunster and
Carhampton, King Arthur taming the sea-serpent; at
Watchet (outside Exmoor but its natural port), St
Decuman crossing from Wales on a hurdle and
miraculously surviving martyrdom; at Minehead,
the whistling ghost of Mistress Leakey; at Leigh
Barton (SS 025359), the tragic figure of Philip Powell,

Badgworthy Water, dividing Somerset from Devon, and leading to the valley of the Doones.

put to death at Tyburn at the close of the Civil War; smugglers at Heddon's Mouth and Trentishoe; at Porlock, the malicious ghost of Lucote; and at Sandhill, near Withycombe, the irrepressible ghost of the thrice-married Joan Carne in the days of James I. And in further proof of the tenacity of tradition, Cecil Sharp, coming to Porlock in search of folk songs in the early 1900s, found them singing of a girl captured and carried off to sea by Danish raiders. That happened in the year 988.

But the supreme legend of Exmoor is of course that of the Doones, and it may be asked how seriously the legend should be taken and what degree of credence it merits. The answer is: a great deal. Richard Blackmore's *Lorna Doone* is a romance, not a history, but the frontiers of the twin kingdoms of Romance and Popular History are ill-defined, each holding enclaves in the other. Blackmore may have created his heroine from the mere hint of a 'hapless maid' (his own words) brought up in the midst of outlaws – but others of the protagonists are as solid flesh and blood as D'Artagnan, Richelieu and Louis XIII in *The Three Musketeers*. Blackmore did not invent the Doones; he gathered together and incorporated into his romance the stories of a robber band on Exmoor that had been current in the district since the seventeenth century, stories written down, in fact, by North Devon schoolgirls in 1853 and embodying popular traditions retailed through five or six generations. He added much more from his own imagination, creating characters out of mere names and incorporating other legendary figures and happenings into his story; for example the resourceful and attractive folk-hero, Tom Faggus, the blacksmith turned highwayman, from South Molton.

Blackmore felt mildly aggrieved that the popularity of *Lorna Doone* should have obscured the merit of his other works with an Exmoor setting, but he made no attempt to intervene in petty disputes over the authenticity or otherwise of the literary background. Only a few months after his death in 1900 an article in the *West Somerset Free Press* created a sensation. A Miss Ida Marie Browne, writing under the pen-name of Audrie Doon and claiming descent by her mother from the Scots family of that name, told readers of a tradition current in the family for two hundred years: that a Sir Ensor Doone, driven out of Scotland by the Earl of Huntley in the year 1618, had been attainted with outlawry and denied a hearing by James I. He took refuge with his wife, sons and a faithful retainer 'in the most remote district they could discover, . . . the bare plains of Exmoor.' Here they stayed for seventy years, terrorising the neighbourhood as in the legends, till in 1699 a descendant of the Earl of Huntley in a gesture of goodwill invited Sir Ensor's descendants to return to Scotland and receive compensation for their long exile. Some of the names in Audrie Doon's account tallied with those in Blackmore, and she also claimed that the family owned a few relics of Exmoor origin and a diary. An independent expert examined these and believed them genuine; whereupon the Muse of Comedy, reluctant to have the question settled, produced an ace from her sleeve and set fire to the study where the artefacts and diary were stored.

So – happily, you may think – we still have no documentary proof of the historicity of the Doones, though I have found a lingering Doon in the Selworthy parish register of the 1750s. It is no great problem to disentangle the inventions from the original in *Lorna Doone* – if you think it matters. The existence of the robber band is beyond doubt, wherever they may have come from and whoever they may have been; and those who follow the 'Doone Trail' or the tracks of Tom Faggus may be confident that they are not treading in the intangible footsteps of a ghost.

As to the questions, which some may judge naïve, 'Why is *Lorna Doone* so popular? Why has it been filmed so many times?', I can only return the equally naïve answers, 'Because it is alive; because the characters live and speak; because they live in the

open air and their lives respond to the changing
seasons; because good overcomes evil; because, in
short, *Lorna Doone* is a heartfelt and beautiful book.'

Despite the changes of the past hundred years,
despite the easing of the conditions of life, the
mobility and increased social intercourse, despite
the immigration, many human types of the old
Exmoor remain – and more than remain, they
flourish. Modern life and education may have
blunted some of the asperities of behaviour and
softened the tang of their speech, but many
characters and types from Exmoor's past have not
only imprinted themselves in popular legend and
the collective mind, they can still be met with, if in
milder forms, in the villages and markets of the
moor and vale.

The temptation is strong to write at length on
these old-time characters, but it must be resisted,
and I will content myself with a passing glance at
some whose lives you will find recounted in greater
detail elsewhere – for Exmoor has been and is
written about more fully and constantly than any
other rural area of comparable size in this country.

We may as well begin, if not chronologically, with
Sir Thomas Dyke Acland III and IV, the figures
distinguishing them from four other baronets of the
same name who could, in the heyday of their family,
ride on their own land from Tiverton to the Bristol
Channel.

Sir Thomas III has gone down in legend as the
wearer of a beaver hat inherited from his father Sir
Thomas II in 1795 and worn year in year out, fair
weather and foul, until shortly before his own death
in 1869, when he relinquished it, as he said, 'not
from any desire to be fashionable (but) because it is
incapable of being any longer repaired. When I am
gone, I anticipate that my successor will be unduly
agitated between sentiment and the sense of
decency, and to save him the pain I now decide to
abandon its use.' But nature lovers have more cause
to remember him – maybe negatively – for having
sold his Forest holdings to John Knight and – very
positively indeed – for having, in the words of an
enthusiast, 'brought the family to the highest
pinnacle of fame as good landlords' and planted the
best part of a million trees, mainly broad-leaves, on
his estates.

Sir Thomas IV, his son, a public figure from duty
rather than inclination, could not, for that reason,
spend so much time on his estates and had to leave
the management to the agents and stewards. These

Dunster Castle and the River Avill. The Castle, once an important stronghold and captured for Parliament by Robert Blake in the Civil War, was rebuilt and modernised in the mid-nineteenth century. It remained in the possession of the Luttrell family from 1376 until 1976, when it was taken over by the National Trust.

were capable and trusted, but the practice brought the comment from an ancient tenant, 'Zur Tummus I do knaw is a vury gude zort o' feller, but . . . but 'tis the devils that be about 'en!' All the same, he commanded immense respect, studied science to improve his land and wrote a book on *The Chemistry of Farming for Small Farmers*. He was almost an exact contemporary of William Ewart Gladstone. They were born and died within a fortnight of each other and followed the same political pilgrimage from Tory to Liberal and then to Home Rule. They were personal friends, and Sir Thomas was a Privy Councillor and served in Gladstone's third administration. Mr and Mrs Gladstone visited his home at Holnicote, near Selworthy, in 1877 and planted two trees. Mrs Gladstone's blew down some time later, but the Grand Old Man's tree flourished and may still be seen beside the public path south of Holnicote House.

I must regretfully pass over the Luttrells of Dunster, the Civil War siege of their castle by Robert Blake, their civic and maritime enterprise, their later involvement in the politics of democracy; nor can I write at length of the Trevelyans of

Nettlecombe Court, of Sir John in the early nineteenth century, his friendship with Clara and the Novellos, and the Coach Road, still visible, which he built to drive all round his estate, or Sir Walter, scholar, editor, vigorous temperance advocate and, by that token, builder of commodious farm cottages and a community hall which stand to-day; or Margaret Trevelyan, brave-hearted, resourceful and tragic heroine of the Civil War.

Hardihood, ingenuity and vigour – these qualities have characterized the men and women of the moor, whether native or adopted settlers; and one may take a small number as exemplary of their trades and callings. As a farmer of an earlier generation, there comes to mind Tom Robbins, known for his authority and the respect he inspired as the 'Emperor of Exmoor' and hill-farming representative of the National Farmers' Union in London in wartime, initiator of beef cattle rearing instead of selling off the calves for veal, treasurer of who knows how many societies and charities, author, shrewd humorist and preserver of the memorials of the past.

As contrast to the settled and rooted inhabitants of Exmoor one might cite the soldier from Cutcombe who led the army of General Wolfe up the midnight precipitous path to the Plains of Abraham; or the traveller and adventurer Aubrey Herbert of Pixton, on the southern fringe of Exmoor, of whom it was written, 'He was careless of his own ease, without fear and without reproach, a hater of tyranny, ever eager to side with the oppressed against the oppressor, a lover of dangerous enterprises, a poet of no mean order, a master of many languages, including Turkish, Arabic, Greek and Albanian, and author of books of great merit, most of them published' – characteristically – 'under a nom de plume.' He lived only from 1880 to 1923, but crowded sixty years of life into his twenty of manhood. He fought in the Balkan Wars of 1911 onwards, won the confidence of the Albanians so completely that after the 1914–1918 War he was twice offered – and refused – the throne of their country; and in the war itself he was so active in extra-diplomatic affairs in the Middle East that some have taken him as the original of John Buchan's Greenmantle.

From Exmoor came two other men whose influence has been world-wide and whose lives have been re-examined and stood the test: Sir George Williams, founder of the YMCA, born at

Ashway Farm, near Dulverton; and Ernest Bevin, born in a labourer's cottage at Winsford, Minister of Labour between 1940 and 1945 and perhaps supremely responsible for his nation's war effort, and later Secretary for Foreign Affairs and architect of NATO.

No account of Exmoor can exclude the story of the lifeboatmen of Lynmouth, called out to launch their *Louisa* on a night of howling storm in 1898 to rescue a ship in distress. Unable to get her into the water, they hauled her for eleven hours of the long winter night over the rough coastlong track up Countisbury Hill, across the Moor and down Porlock Hill, to launch her at the Weir, then rowed back along the rock-bound coast and brought the shipwrecked Spanish sailors safe to shore.

Exmoor, however, has never lacked characters to act as a counter-poise to the public-spirited and heroic, and the nineteenth-century clergy furnish a veritable portrait gallery of colourful, vigorous characters of an everyday toughness and hardihood it takes an effort to comprehend today. The best known must be 'Jack' Russell of Swimbridge, whose name has of course been preserved by the terriers he bred; but who gained celebrity as the better type of 'hunting parson', one who hunted every weekday during the 'season' but knew all his parishoners by name and attended to his parsonical duties conscientiously according to his lights. Russell's rides regularly took him fifty, sixty, seventy miles a day. To attend a meet in West Somerset he would ride the thirty miles of rough moorland track to the Anchor Hotel at Porlock Weir, kept by the sportsman Jim Goddard, and consume a leg of mutton and two bottles of port for his dinner. Next morning he would start out early for the meet perhaps ten miles away, hunt all day with the hounds and ride home thirty or more miles to Swimbridge the same night.

A more complex character altogether than this hard-riding old sportsman was Parson Jack Froude. Knowstone, where he lorded it for half a century, is a pleasant little spot nowadays, on the southern fringe of the moor, but in Froude's time it was regarded as remote and the inhabitants half-civilized. The parish suited him well, for the remoteness from bishops and their visitations gave him freedom to act pretty well as he liked.

He came from a distinguished family, with one brother a famous historian, but he himself, not to gloss over it, was a ruffian and a bully, though a

Porlock Weir – opening the sluice gates. These in fact constitute the 'weir', an enclosed harbour. Once a busy if small trading port, Porlock Weir now accommodates pleasure craft almost exclusively.

courageous rider and physically as hard as chilled steel. He was an excellent judge of horse and hound, and as he had private means he kept his own pack and hunted whenever, wherever and whatever he could. However, Froude was his own law. He ruled the roost and had a bevy of almost feudal retainers who would carry out his wishes from waylaying bishops to burning hayricks.

I would not claim that everyone on Exmoor has taken the life and the characters of the past into their consciousness. Most men and women are not made like that, the present and the future take up their attention; but our ancestors and predecessors have shaped both our physical and our moral and spiritual world. We may forget or ignore them; that is our loss. To know them, to find more about them, to understand the parts they have played in the shaping of our world, that is all gain.

10 **Exmoor wildlife**

A hundred books could not contain all the wealth of information that exists concerning the flora and fauna of Exmoor, and this chapter is intended only as the briefest of guides. A total of 243 species of bird has been seen on Exmoor with more than one hundred nesting in the park each year. Nearly all are protected by law, and to kill them or take their eggs and young is a punishable offence. The barn owl, kingfisher, merlin, peregrine falcon and sparrowhawk have even greater protection and their nests must not be disturbed or even photographed without the appropriate permit. However, the number of flowers, grasses and trees on and around the Moor far surpasses the number of birds. Since 1974 the Exmoor Natural History Society has located and recorded over 900 species of flowers and grasses locally, from Abraham-Isaac-and-Jacob to Yarrow, Yellow-wort and Yew, with Zanichellia (horned pondweed) thrown in for good measure, and Zizania (darnel) no doubt waiting to creep in as soon as the farmer's back is turned. But what of the habitats for this wealth of wildlife?

There are five main ones: the open moorland of both grass and heather, which for many visitors is the essence of Exmoor; the woodlands; the lowland villages and farmlands which extend up the wider valleys and on to the lower moor; the combes and river valleys, and the coastline with its soaring cliffs and rounded hillsides dropping down to the sea. For all these areas, the climate tends to be rather wet and severe, though less so than in the north of England, with winds from the south west predominant. In winter the snowfalls can be spectacular, spurred on by strong winds and the open character of the land, although the valleys also receive their share of snow which can remain there long after the higher moorland is clear. The Vale of Porlock and the coastal fringes tend to be milder, with the north-facing cliffs sheltered from the prevailing wind, unlike the more rugged coastlines of other parts of north Devon and Cornwall which have to contend with Atlantic gales.

Nearly all the open moorland lies over the 1,000

Western gorse.

Winsford Hill looking towards Dunkery, heather retreating and gorse invading.

foot contour, the line to which the mist most often comes down. The Brendon Hills reach 1,300 feet and Dunkery somewhat over 1,700 feet.

To put the matter another way and locate the main vegetation cover, which only partly depends on the geology, Exmoor may be seen as a series of broad plateaux roughly parallel with the coast and separated from one another by the valleys of the East and West Lyn, the Exe and the Barle, though at the western end of the Moor the highland is continuous. The areas richest in heather and ling – if rich is the word for plants which, though among the most beautiful on the Moor, enjoy only a brief glory in late summer before subsiding into their winter greyish-brown – are Hangman, Trentishoe, the Valley of Rocks, Porlock Common, North Hill, Brendon Common, Dunkery, Winsford Hill, Withypool Common, Molland and Anstey Commons. (The Brendon Hills have none to speak of.) Although the open heathland may look wild and natural, it is largely a man-made landscape. Until prehistoric times the high land was sparsely covered with trees and man's subsequent clearing, grazing and burning has prevented tree regeneration. The areas of heather moorland all lie

outside the Forest boundary; within it, very little heather grows and coarse purple moor grass predominates. The reason for this absence is not very clear. One theory is that heather is the natural cover, and that where cultivation has been attempted and then abandoned, heather returns (in point of fact, if the ground is fairly well drained, bracken may invade)) but, the theory goes on, heavy over-grazing in the old days destroyed the heather, and the coarse grass took over completely and ineradicably. As a positive example, Dunkery is heath-covered, and this is an area which surely has never been heavily grazed or under the plough.

Apart from the heather (mainly ling, bell heather and cross-leaved heath in damp places), the moorland is home to bilberry – whortleberry is the local name – which has dark purple fruit in late summer. In early summer yellow patches of gorse can be seen in many places, although some gorse flowers all year long. Smaller plants to look for include tormentil, milkwort, eyebright and blue heath speedwell while damper places will have ivy-leaved bellflower, heath spotted orchid, bog pimpernel and the insect-eating western butterwort. The moorland west of Dunkery is a good place to see many of these plants, as well as the area around Pinkworthy Pond, which is now owned by the National Park. If you are looking for a quiet place up on the moor, away from it all, Exe Head is the home of silence.

The whortleberry grows in profusion on the heathland, and with clotted cream is one of Exmoor's finest delicacies.

Commonest of the falcons, the kestrel yet compels admiration by his mastery of hovering.

While out on the Moor watch out for birds of prey such as the buzzard which frequents the combes leading to the moorland. Kestrels and sparrowhawks are also fairly common, but you would be lucky to catch sight of the elusive merlin although it does breed in eastern combes. Other birds likely to be seen include curlew and raven, which winter on the Moor, and summer residents such as ring ouzels, wheatears, whinchats, tree pipits and willow warblers.

But the creature most associated with the Moor must be the Exmoor pony. He comes of ancient stock. One of the duties of the Free Suitors, as mentioned earlier, was to round up the 'equas silvestras' (wild horses) – several hundred of them. The ponies of today, however, are all descended from a herd of twenty, the Anchor Herd of Ashway Farm, saved when the Forest was sold off by the Crown.

The isolation of Exmoor from outlandish influences kept the native breed remarkably pure until the twentieth century, when breeding control took over. The ponies are no longer truly wild nowadays, they all belong to someone, but they still wander and graze on the Moor the year round. Today there are more than twenty herds in Britain, and six of these on Exmoor are privately run. In 1980 the Park Authority, concerned that the breed might be declining, bought three filly foals and two yearling fillies as foundation stock for their herd of pure-bred Exmoor ponies. In the following spring they were turned out on to Haddon Hill, an area of 400 acres above Wimbleball reservoir. They thrived, and their well-being was regularly checked by a visiting shepherd. A five-year-old stallion, Loganberry, joined them, and just before the birth of the first foal one group was moved to Warren Farm; so now, at Warren and Haddon Hill, the National Park Authority is running two herds in support of the breed.

Pure-bloodedness in any pony implies characteristic features or points, and these make the Exmoor pony an attractive animal. He is larger than the Shetland but still stands only twelve to thirteen hands high, with a reddish to dark coat, proof against the deluges and rigours of winter on the exposed moorland. He feeds on heather, gorse, bracken, tubers and molinia grass, and needs no extra provender.

His 'toad' eye, despite the name, is 'full and kind, and slightly hooded and set under a jutting brow

which throws off the rain.' His strong head and short pointed ears mark him out as dependable, and he is even-tempered and far less prone to nervous spasms, stage fright and equine epilepsy than his Anglo-Arab cousins. As well as the herds named above you may see others on Winsford Hill, Ashway Side, Molland Common, Codsend Moor and Withypool Common, but not on the mainly enclosed Brendon Hills.

While out on the Moor you may catch a glimpse of another of Exmoor's well-known animals – the red deer – which moves between the Moor and neighbouring woodlands. Only four of the forty species of deer in the world roam Exmoor, and three of them – the fallow, roe and sika deer – are intruders; but the fourth, the red deer, belongs here. He is the native, he makes free of all that Exmoor has to offer, and he stands head and shoulders – literally – above the deer of all the other species.

From time immemorial the red deer has been accounted the monarch of the Forest, and even nowadays he shares the condition of a monarch, being the object of adulation for a sizeable part of the nation, ogled by others, chivvied and chased by

Exmoor ponies are companionable creatures in the wild, and should not be kept in solitary state.

others again, and with little chance of completely escaping the importunate, the well-wishing or the plain ill-intentioned.

Epicures to a fault, the deer delight in fresh shoots of saplings, cider apples, heather, bramble, ivy and corn, acorns, berries, birch and beech leaves; but root crops are especially prized by the cognoscenti, who raid clamps when desperate and at other times make themselves destructively free of the turnip fields, taking only one bite at a root before moving on to the next. An enterprising stag can, it is alleged, ruin an acre of root crops in a night; but in general the farmers who support the hunt tolerate this otherwise intolerable intruder, in the hope of running him to his death on the open moor.

No other aspect of Exmoor life, not even moorland reclamation, arouses such passion as the hunting of the wild red deer. That attests its hold, and to write objectively invites a charge of commitment to 'the other side'. To condemn the hunt marks one down as an urban ignoramus; to support it brands one as a rural cut-throat. It has to be said, however, that all parties to the dispute – except the one at the centre – agree that someone must aid nature in her task of natural selection by culling the deer. If man does not thin out their numbers, starvation will. The argument rages over the method: which – hunting or shooting – is the more effective, inflicts less suffering on the deer and offers the better safeguard against poaching and wholesale slaughter by aggrieved agriculturalists. But there is also a moral question to arouse the passions; should one species of animal, for the sake of the pleasure that some people find in hunting, be

A meet of the Devon and Somerset Staghounds. Colour photographs of the later stages of the hunt are not easily come by.

denied the protection against cruelty given to all the others? And should any organization be allowed to organize the hunting and death of an animal in order to give enjoyment to sportspeople and spectators?

Three packs of staghounds hunt Exmoor today: the Tiverton, Quantock and Devon and Somerset ('D and S'); but hunting, as we have seen, has been carried on – with interruptions – ever since Saxon days. Originally deer were hunted for meat and royal sport, now it is for more popular sport, and venison is the by-product. But that simplifies the question, because the deer, for all their beauty, ravage the crops, and many farmers, as stated above, only tolerate this for the excitement of joining in the hunt.

Unquestionably hunting enjoys very considerable support on Exmoor, but there is also disapproval, though strong social pressures make the degree of opposition hard to judge.

On the credit side, however, there should be placed a considerable number of events indirectly connected with the hunt out of season, that is, in the summer, which, for their glimpses into Exmoor, it would be a pity to miss: Exford Horse Show in August, where you may see the best of the Exmoor pony breed; Dunster Show, 130 years strong and attracting thousands of visitors, competitors and exhibitors from a radius of over a hundred miles; and gymkhanas in different villages of the moor.

But the red stag, despite all hazards, is every inch a king. He stands, when well grown, some forty-four inches at the shoulder – the hinds are about six inches less – and when he stretches his full height to survey his kingdom, his antlers top six feet. And it is of course the antlers, or 'head', which give him the regal air and they are borne by the male alone. He sheds and renews them every year and, remarkably, sixteen to eighteen weeks suffice to grow the 'head' in all its majesty. As S H Burton remarks, 'The production of so great a mass of horn in so short a time is one of nature's marvels.'

Richard Jefferies acutely observed that the stag grows his antlers in time with the 'brake fern', the bracken. When the green shoot rises from the earth it shapes itself into a coil or question mark as if in bemused protest at finding itself exposed to the April chill. At the same time, from the second year onward, the stag's antlers begin to grow. He has none until a year old, but between one and two years he grows a knob of bone on either side of his brow, and 'spires', slender upright horns, spring

The head of the male red deer.

from these. In the new growing season every year the new horn is tender, flexible and covered with a skin called the 'velvet', and as long as this remains he is, in theory, protected from hunting, In late July it seems to irritate him and he rubs his head against trees to get rid of the encumbrance. In his third year he grows the brow rights, in his fourth the trey, in his fifth the middle of bay rights, and in his sixth, points atop. From his fifth year he is accounted 'warrantable', fit for hunting, but he devotes the next six or seven years, if he lives as long, to perfecting the masterpiece, adding more points atop and increasing the size, strength, solidity and serrations – for the antlers are more than an ornament, they are a powerful weapon, and he wields them vigorously against his rivals in the rutting season, and defends himself desperately against man and hound when brought to bay.

After the twelfth year he declines into the cervine equivalent of the lean and slippered pantaloon; but in his prime he justifies Richard Jefferies' tribute: 'There is no more beautiful creature than a stag in his pride of antler, his coat of ruddy gold, his grace of form and motion. He seems the natural owner of the ferny combes, the oak woods, the broad slopes of heather. They belong to him, and he steps upon the sward in lordly mastership.'

The deer are shy creatures, with good reason. The Moor holds 700 or 800 of them, but to see them in any number you have to know where to look, and not even the trained huntsman or 'stag harbourer' always knows for certain. Their only enemy is man, and for preference they hide in woodland coverts during the day but come out in the evening, usually in small herds, to browse and graze in the open. They favour the old oak woodlands of steep-sided combes and river valleys, particularly the Dunkery region above Horner Water and its head tributaries, but they may be seen – or nine times out of ten, not seen – in any place where these conditions obtain. Other herds regularly inhabit Hawkcombe, Grabbist behind Minehead, Worthy and Culbone Woods, Croydon Hill and above Badgworthy.

The mating season, or 'rut', begins in late September, when the stag herds break up and the individual members set about rounding up as many hinds, with their three-month old calves, as they can collect or hold. In this season the stag can be dangerous, not only to his rivals with whom he fights to blood, but also to incautious humans. His whole demeanour, writes S H Burton, 'changes from the usual timidity to the fierce bearing and aggressive restlessness of the mating season. . . . Mute for eleven months of the year, the stag makes up for his long silence in October. The noise, or 'belling', is difficult to describe: something between the bellow of a bull and the roar of a lion, trailing off into a coughing grunt, a weird sound in a lonely combe, especially after dark.'

Monarch of the forest indeed, and like a monarch of the Restoration he takes his seraglio with him wherever he goes.

In contrast to the red deer, fallow deer – descended from escapers from the deer parks at Dunster Castle and Nettlecombe Court – are much less numerous; but small herds may be seen in the plantations on Croydon Hill or eastwards to Monksilver.

The roe deer – woodland creatures who browse on shrubs and tips of young trees – have spread from Dorset and Hampshire, and have been seen in the Haddeo Valley, on the Brendons and in Selworthy Woods. The sika deer – offspring of escapers from Pixton, Dulverton – frequent the woods of the Mole and Bray valleys on the southern fringes of Exmoor.

'Forest', on Exmoor, does not mean forest in the usual sense, and mention has been made of the process by which the original wooded cover of the high moor was reduced and eventually annihilated. In the more favourable climate of the valleys, however, trees held their own, and the oak and beech in particular were valued for their contribution to the food of the herds of swine. To judge by Domesday Book, the main areas of woodland a thousand years ago were along the northern coast and combes, especially around Porlock, the main river valleys and the northern slopes of the Brendon Hills; but the upland, bare of trees, served as a hunting ground for the king, where he could pursue the deer and other animals roused from their valley woodland coverts.

The early English people – as we may call the merging Saxons and British in the years before the Norman Conquest, built in wood rather than stone, and their woodcraft was well developed. They understood the art of coppicing, a process described by Roger Miles in his *Trees and Woods of Exmoor:*

> 'Coppicing is obtained by cutting down a tree and allowing the several shoots which spring from the stump (or stool) to grow for a period of time – seven to thirty years appear to have been the approximate limits but they varied according to site, species and intended use. . . . The systematic cropping of oak coppices for charcoal, tan bark, fuel and a wide variety of local uses became established as a local style of woodland management from the Middle Ages up to and including much of the nineteenth century.'

We have seen how by a strange miscalculation, the need for heavy shipbuilding timber brought the old Forest to an end, but in time the trees began to return to Exmoor. Both John and Frederic Knight planted trees in the form of windbreaks around the farms they created and in the beech plantation – despite the name – of Birch Cleave at Simonsbath, the latter with the idea of establishing a nursery for beech seedlings to be planted on the bank surrounding the Forest. In the great estates of the lowlands around the moor, however, there was already a long tradition of planting, an activity

which reached its height in the eighteenth century. Today, in a countryside which is being laid bare, we are paying the price of two centuries' subsequent neglect. Nevertheless, we must record our debt of gratitude to the Trevelyans of Nettlecombe, the Caernarvons of Pixton, the Luttrells of Dunster, the Hallidays of Glenthorne and most of all to the Aclands, whose lands extended from Killerton near Exeter to the shores of Exmoor. They planted with imagination and an eye to beauty. Their woods in the Horner Valley and on the southern side of North Hill above Selworthy contain miles of pleasant, shaded walks and rides, with many varieties of beautiful trees as well as the traditional oak and beech: ash, chestnut, holm-oak (ilex), sycamore and walnut and, among the conifers, larch, Scots and Corsican pine.

Much of the former Acland land is now the property of the National Trust, thanks to the gift of Sir Richard Acland in 1944. The Trust now controls some 2,000 acres of woods, including the scientifically important Horner Woods in the Somerset part of the park, and has acquired or controls Watersmeet, Woody Bay and the Heddon Valley in the Devon part – all sites of special scientific interest . There is access for the public along the paths and rides,

Birch Cleave, Simonsbath, early morning.

There is also a tenuous connection between the activities of the National Trust and the Forestry Commission, in that Sir Richard Acland's father, Francis, played an important part in the formation of that Commission in 1919. The Forestry Commission has incurred heavy criticism – some would say 'has provoked it' – for its policy of concentrating on conifers and neglecting hardwoods, but it must be recognized that this was its remit, to build up a stock of quick-growing timber to make good the depletion of war and provide for emergencies. Nevertheless, the 3,000 acres of conifers sprawling across the northern slopes of the Brendon Hills and Croydon Hill disfigure, for most people, a beautiful landscape. To be fair, it should be acknowledged that the stated attitude of the Commission has considerably changed and the idea of a protected screen of hardwood trees is now accepted, but the idea is not too readily translated into reality.

The continuing problem is that of beauty versus commerce, and it has been exacerbated by the arrival of commercial forestry syndicates wishing to buy up old, mature woodlands, stripping them and replanting with conifers. The National Park Authority, aware of the threat, placed conservation orders on 700 acres in the Somerset part – at Grabbist, Kingsdown Clump, Birch Cleave, Hawkcombe, Glenthorne and part of the Blathwayt Estate's Porlock woods; but this represented only a small part of the 6,000 acres graded for landscape value. Nevertheless, it was a start, and Somerset County Council stepped in to buy large areas where the syndicates would not agree to compromise on planting; on North Hill, Minehead and most of Hawkcombe. Thus over a thousand acres of woodland are now – happily, we hope – held in trust for the public and managed by the National Park Authority, with a tree nursery at Bossington.

Despite the large areas of woodland and moor, most of Exmoor is farmland, with stone walls and hedgebanks separating the fields. The high plateau is dominated by old beech hedgerows, remnants of moorland enclosures during the late nineteenth and early twentieth centuries. Hedgerows in fields and beside roads and old lanes are home to a variety of flowering plants, most of them familiar species likely to be found in other parts of England. However, look out for the wall pennywort on drier banks – it is common on Exmoor but rare elsewhere. In contrast to birds, which tend to stay more or less in one type of habitat, animals will

The pennywort, also known as the navelwort, grows commonly on old walls and banks throughout the national park except the high land of the centre and east. It was recorded in Turner's 'Herball' from Somerset in 1562. Its cousin, the marsh pennywort, grows mainly in the centre and south.

move from farmland to the woods and on to the moorland, using the edges of each area. Along with small mammals, Exmoor has its share of foxes, which will even venture boldly at night into the streets of Lynton, Porlock and Minehead; and badgers, which make their setts for preference on sloping ground to avoid flooding, in deciduous woodland, thick hedgerows or overgrown quarries. Badgers are nocturnal animals and therefore unlikely to be seen by a casual walker, but their nightly forays lead them across roads and all too often they fall victim to the motor car – for which reason they need your extra caution when driving at night.

It has been estimated that there are more than three hundred miles of rivers and streams on Exmoor, with even the larger rivers, the Exe and the Barle, having their source high up on the moors. The streams run down narrow combes or valleys, often through woodland in their lower reaches. Time spent exploring these streams will be rewarded by the sight of riverside plants and birds. Visit Farley Water for a glimpse of dipper, chiff-chaff, wagtail, stonechat and redstart, or the Lower Barle with the addition of heron and kingfisher.

Oare weed, The Gore, Porlock Weir, at low tide.

Cloutsham Gate provides stream habitats mixed with woods and farmland and a good variety of birds as a result. If, while beside a stream, you should chance upon one of the few remaining otters of Exmoor – perhaps twenty all told – enjoy your privileged glimpse but remember that the otter, after being hounded and persecuted for generations, is at last protected by the law from those who would gladly continue his persecution. The Somerset Trust for Nature Conservation and the National Park Authority would be glad to know of your otter in order to safeguard him, but otherwise ignorance of his habitat offers him the best hope of survival.

The coast is where Exmoor starts, or finishes, depending on the direction in which you are travelling. The Somerset and North Devon Coast Path follows the entire national park coast from Minehead and provides a good base from which to explore this area, The cliffs are home to the colourful thrift or seapink as well as white sea campion, and at Glenthorne you may find the rare silver ragwort on the red sandstone cliffs. Other areas have woodland almost down to the beach, particularly between Foreland Point and Porlock Weir, so providing habitat for woodland plants and birds. Porlock Bay has a shingle bank where you can find the everlasting pea and yellow horned poppy, while on the salt marsh behind the bank are

The guillemot, nesting with the razorbill along the cliffs west of Lynmouth, has increased in numbers from 150 pairs in 1971 to nearly 500 individual birds in 1986.

sea beet, glasswort and saltwort. Even the water
ditches at Porlock Bay have their share of plants
such as arrowhead, bur marigold, yellow flag and a
variety of rushes. Other areas. such as North Hill,
have moorland vegetation up to the top of the cliffs,
providing a link with the moorland to the south.
Exmoor's coast has its share of sea birds –
guillemots and razorbills for example – and from
Lynmouth there are boat trips to view the cliffs and
their birds from the best vantage point – the sea.

11 **Farming on the Moor**

Exmoor, like the people who live there, has alternately resisted and accepted change, but over the past thirty or forty years the pace has quickened. Each of the individual changes in the landscape and pattern of farming has affected only a small section of the Moor, but taken in all they have given it a very different aspect from the early years of this century. The 'hills of great height covered with heather' of which Richard Jefferies wrote in 1883 have lost much of their purple colouring. The heather, though still plentiful in certain parts, has retreated, and on Winsford Hill for example, gorse or 'vuzz' has begun to invade. Why?

This takes us to the heart of the question of moorland farming.

Unlike the lowlander, the hill farmer of Exmoor is mainly concerned with stock-rearing and grazing,

This field of stooked oats is a heart-warming sight, but rare even on Exmoor.

and this makes his economic existence far more precarious. He only sells once a year, and he must pit his experience and wit against recurring but unpredictable emergencies. He has little capital to help him weather a storm, and can only have recourse to a cut-back on the costs within his control or to a small improvement of rough grazing.

In recent years, however, economic forces have brought him help from the unexpected quarter of the lowlands. Development prompted by greed is devouring our best farmland faster than ever before and exerting indirect pressure on the hill farmer to send his half-raised stock to the lowland farms for finishing, so that their loss of good land may be compensated for by the greater productivity involved by the 'finishing' process. This is where the hill farmer benefits. His rough grazings have been called the nursery of beef and sheep production, for two-thirds of the sheep breeding flock of the country are his, and almost a half of the lambs and a quarter of the cattle slaughtered have come from his raising. His stock are only moderately efficient protein-producers, but they can graze and browse contentedly on grass or heather during the short growing season; and when that is over, the excess stock – those which would over-graze the moor in the winter – are sold down to the lowlands for finishing and fattening more rapidly in those favourable conditions and fertility. Both farmers gain, for a lowland acre used for eighteen-month beef would yield 400 lb; but when used for finishing hill-reared calves, the yield shoots up to 650 lb, not significantly below the 700 lb of baconer carcase that would have come from an acre of barley for feeding the hyper-efficient pig. What is more, the practice also frees precious lowland acres for highly profitable cash crops, and the upland farmer, cheered by hill cow and ewe (or 'yewel') subsidies or 'headage', goes on his way rejoicing; and Mrs Partington, far away from the scene of agricultural action in Brighthelmstone-on-Sea, buys her weekend joint at a price which, all things considered, is virtually derisory.

Exmoor farms, however, do not function as miniatures of Texan ranches or Australian sheep-stations. Their acres are numbered in hundreds, not thousands – four hundred would probably be a high average. But we know that the vegetation cannot compare with that of the valleys, so how do they manage?

One of the great estates, the Fortescue, may be

Exmoor Horn ram,
Pinkworthy.

taken as a good example, since it owes much to the farming pattern established by the Knights. Such an estate will contain many 500-acre blocks of unimproved moorland which are let out to the farms next to them for summer grazing by cattle from mid-May and by ewes after shearing. Generally the stock allowed will depend on the size of the farm; one-and-a-half sheep for every acre of the home farm or a cow and calf for every ten acres. This arrangement works well for the plenty of 'in-bye' (improved) land on the farmer's holding, as having the stock off the premises, so to speak, he can make hay or silage on the in-bye and take the mature animals through the winter.

The grazing of sheep and cattle creates the vegetation pattern of Exmoor, or rather it continues a pattern set by early farmers and kept in balance – if a precarious balance – by the different grazing habits and the custom of swaling or burning.

The livestock of course need to be hardy, resilient and unfastidious, but enterprising enough to search out the better plants, and this role is fulfilled by the traditional hill breeds, especially Galloway cattle and Exmoor Horn and Cheviot ewes. They can last out the winter if need be and thrive where the more productive lowland animals would retire from the fray. But other bulls and rams, as well as those mentioned above to sire the stock for rearing in the lowlands, are foreigners: White Shorthorns, Herefords, Charolais, or Border Leicesters, Scotch Blackfaces, Texel or Dorsets.

The ponies, too, play a part. Most kinds of moorland vegetation figure in their diet, but by eating the gorse while it is still young and tender

Traditional hill cattle
breeds can last out the
winter on the Moor.

they prevent it spreading and colonizing. When visitor and other pressures drive them away, as from Winsford Hill, the gorse advances and the landscape deteriorates with alarming rapidity.

Devon cattle, with swaling in the background.

But even the most insatiable browsers and grazers cannot fully control the pattern of vegetation as the farmer needs it, and he has an extra method, swaling – burning off the excess of the heather and molinia grass. Heather, left to itself, grows stalky and dies away at the centre. Burning, if kept from the roots, keeps the old plants healthy; but with molinia grass the case is otherwise. It dies off in winter, and the surplus growth left after summer grazing clogs soggily together to choke the new growth and smother the better sub-dominant grasses. Burning clears away the nuisance, lets in light and air, and the new grass springs healthy and green.

That is not the only benefit of swaling. Being carried out in the spring, it lessens the risk of a disastrous fire after drought, for the heather will not catch light again until it has grown woody and old, and the molinia has been rid of encumbrance without harm to the parent plants. Moreover, it checks the advance of unwanted plants, keeps down disease by destroying ticks, and produces palatable grazing for both farm stock and wildlife. The work of swaling has to be compressed into a mere month or so, for the molinia is generally too wet to burn before the end of February and the official period ends on 31st March; but the earlier the burning, the better for the new growth; necessity becomes a virtue and farmer, livestock, moor and wildlife all gain.

Such a delicate balance of interests, such co-operation of man with nature, such a partnership of interests between hill and lowland, between great estates and adjacent farms, present an image pleasing to the onlooker, but is it true?

Sadly it represents an ideal once achieved, honoured by long usage but eventually, within our own recent time, subjected to economic pressures and giving way before them.

The changes in farming practice since 1950 and the wholesale ploughing, enclosure and fencing of the 1960s, have been mentioned elsewhere in this book. What has not been mentioned is the lamentable long-term result of the policy of subsidies for stock rearing and other premiums of suckler cows and sheep, especially fat lambs. As sheep farming has become more profitable the number of hill farms has diminished, largely because the farmer with more land and more stock, and therefore a higher income from subsidies and sales, fares disproportionately better than the smaller man because his business costs disproportionately less to run. Agricultural contractors have taken over from the old full-time farm worker or labourer, mechanization favours the larger farmer, he can better afford winter shelter for his stock, and his bank manager is captivated by his ability to repay a very substantial loan. So now, when the lease of a small farm runs out, the landlord may take over, merge the land with a neighbouring farm to double its size, turn the farmhouse into a mere private residence or 'second home' – and the hundred-acre man with generations of farming skill is lost to Exmoor.

And now, undermining the situation still further, food surpluses in the EEC and the withdrawal of subsidies for ploughing have dealt the Exmoor farmer a shrewd blow. With the prop of his modest prosperity knocked away, what hope remains for him? He knows that surpluses may one day give way to shortages, but he cannot plan and invest for

Sheep drenching on Mannacot Farm.

so uncertain a happening, for agriculture demands continuity, even though its environment – heat, cold, rain, snow and hail – suffers daily and hourly change. It also demands responsibility, and responsibility implies farming with a care for the long-term well-being of the land – and one unpleasant fact should not be glossed over : the effect of the EEC's system of payment by 'headage'. Since the number of beasts is the deciding factor, the unscrupulous and irresponsible farmer is encouraged to overstock; the Moor becomes overgrazed, his beasts become underfed, and both moor and livestock suffer. Such farmers form a small minority but a significant one, since their irresponsibility has caused disproportionate harm.

But for any Exmoor farmer, as far ahead as he can see, farming will not pay as it has done, and an agriculture in distress means an ailing national park. He urgently needs to know what profitable activities he can take up to compensate for what he has lost. Tourism, of course, or the last ditch expedient of converting his barns into holiday accommodation, serves one, but only one, of the purposes for which the national park was designated. Some, more enterprising, would hope to find ways of using the resources native to the district – timber, rocks and water-power – to revive and re-create its many skills and arts. Others again would say, 'We see our future in finding new ways to develop the old farming, to conserve what is best of our environment and' – quoting from the duties laid upon the Park Authority – 'to enhance the natural beauty of Exmoor.'

12 **The national park today**

Like all industrious and successful organizations, the Exmoor National Park Authority has never lacked critics. Some impartial onlookers may think that the louder the criticism, the better the organization is doing its job. That is not necessarily true. Effective action can silence criticism, and the Authority, when faced with a problem or a challenge, has always chosen first the way of reason and, where possible, conciliation; and by dint of thirty years' patient persuasion and active work for the economy of Exmoor it has gained acceptance and respect. On Exmoor these do not come easily.

Critics, in the nature of things, will still delight to bark and bite. They did so even before Parliament designated the park in 1954. The two county councils opposed it, the rural district councils opposed it, the government inspector

Entering Exmoor National Park near East Anstey Common.

recommended against it and the Minister wrote to his officials, 'What can be the use of a national park on Exmoor? There may be enough parks already.' The national park lobby, small but vocal, would not give up, and the Government yielded and designated Exmoor as a national park run by three separate bodies, the two county councils retaining their control and a joint committee with advisory powers only.

To compound the difficulties, the National Parks Commission, which was to become the Countryside Commission, could happily and usefully advise but had no power to impose its will on determined agricultural developers. All in all, this troika-with-back-seat-driver arrangement served excellently to create bureaucratic delay and was practically useless for protecting the Moor against the changes gathering momentum to sweep across it.

As the 1960s wore on and wire fences crept over the Moor and increasingly the heathland was converted, diverted or perverted to grazing, the failure of a purely advisory role became distressingly obvious. But 'relief and enlargement' came from an unexpected quarter. The 1974 local government reorganization, so unwanted, so perversely imposed, so wounding to local pride, also established a new National Park Authority, for the first time with a home and base of operations within the park itself, at Dulverton. The Authority took over the offices of the dissolved Dulverton Rural District Council, originally the early Victorian workhouse, a dignified two-storey classical building with an elegant louvred wooden lantern. From there it has worked efficiently and effectively and gained willing co-operation from the large majority of the local community – and that seems the best point to outline the work which the National Park Authority undertakes.

With a small specialist staff at Exmoor House, headed by the National Park Officer, it has the oversight of 265 square miles of varied countryside subject to increasing pressures for development. The National Park Officer reports to a committee made up of eight county councillors from Somerset, four from Devon, one district councillor each from North Devon and West Somerset and seven other members appointed for their special interests or knowledge by the Secretary of State for the Environment.

Like every other Park Authority, the Exmoor Committee has the task of preserving and

Exmoor House, built as a Poor Law institution, adapted as the offices of the Dulverton Rural District Council and now (since 1973) the headquarters of the National Park Authority.

enhancing the natural beauty of the park and promoting its enjoyment by the general public. 'All three at once?' says the cynic, 'surely not.' 'Surely yes,' retorts the Authority, 'and it can be done by planning, conservation, land management and visitor services.'

The Committee is the planning authority for Exmoor, and it is faced with problems different in kind from any that have occurred before. Change and development, modest and gradual until a few years ago, are gathering momentum. Hill country farmers, finding themselves suddenly deprived of some of the subsidies they enjoyed – and needed – are having to seek new sources of income, and these involve new buildings. Unemployment is rife, new industries are required, but these must be on a modest scale suitable to a rural setting. A great many visitors are coming to Exmoor, and they need accommodation. Again new building. But the beauty of Exmoor is fragile, and the wrong siting of a development – even the colour or material of the roof – can cause irreparable damage. The Authority provides guides on such matters for builders, the planning officers advise, recommend and warn –

but it cannot be stated too clearly that in the long run the responsibility for whatever building may strike your eye as a calculated insult to the countryside lies with the members of the Committee.

Planning control seems to its rueful soldiery a form of never-ending guerrilla warfare with occasional small victories, frequent defeats and no certainty of support from the rear echelon, the Department of the Environment; but the National Park Authority has to think strategically. As a committee of Somerset County Council with representation from Devon, it is subject in the long run to the overriding Structure Plans of both, but it nevertheless prepares detailed local plans for whole areas of the park in order to guide future changes and see that the right facilities are provided at the right time.

The problem posed by commercial forestry, with its emphasis on quick-maturing conifers, has been referred to in earlier pages. Sadly, two barely reconcilable philosophies come into play; the enhancement of natural beauty versus commercial profitability, and the Authority has been starved of the powers it should rightfully have to fulfil its planning and controlling role in this important field, Whatever successes it has enjoyed have come from discussion and persuasion. Perhaps the thought sweetens the pill a little, but the invasion of Exmoor and the ousting of the oak and the ash, the birch tree and the beech by regiments of sombre conifers, Nature's Blackshirts, will continue to rankle until the enhancement of natural beauty is permitted by ministerial order to win the day.

The National Park Authority has large holdings of moorland and farmland, notably at Warren Farm, with grazing rights over 880 acres on Larkbarrow. Here it is experimenting with new systems of conservation and land management, swaling only one small area at a time instead of the more wholesale method of tradition. Its task is now to prove that this public involvement and responsibility offer the best hope for the progress and prosperity of the Moor – maybe an uphill task, but the Authority has pioneered in showing, often in the teeth of incomprehension and mistrust, that the maintenance of traditional farming and the conservation of natural beauty can not only be reconciled, but can go forward hand in hand. Inevitably some critics will see in such involvement the menace of 'creeping socialism', but those who detach themselves from narrow dogma will watch

A national park carpenter making a gate.

the Authority with interest and concern and wish it well.

The Authority suffers from chronic under-funding. Every year it conscientiously reviews its needs and commitments according to governmental guidelines, makes its bid for resources and is then short-funded. Sometimes the hard-pressed county councils have made up the deficiency, but their own plight will no longer allow this. Only a change of heart by the government can set the matter right, and few people indulge in any delusion as to the government's heart.

As well as its work on planning control and the conservation of land within the park, the National Park Authority's Visitor Services section works to help Exmoor's two and a half million visitors each year make the most of the national park. In addition to providing picnic sites, view points and car parks, the Authority operates five Information Centres and organizes programmes of guided walks and evening talks during the holiday season.

Young people are not forgotten either. The Youth and Schools branch of Visitor Services helps organizers of school and youth groups to plan study trips to the park and thus learn more about the importance of Exmoor while enjoying themselves. In fact the Exmoor National Park Authority quite obviously spares no pains to make visitors feel at ease, but the staff have also exerted themselves in providing a service which may do little for your ease and comfort but will add most mightily to your enjoyment: the Waymarked Walks. Along 600 miles of footpath – think of that, Land's End to Aberdeen, Calais to Toulon, San Francisco to Salt Lake City –

The National Park has waymarked over 600 miles of Exmoor footpaths, bridleways and byways.

they have set waymarks, dashes of red, yellow or blue, clearly visible but unobtrusive, painted on trees, posts, stakes or cairns – to help you wander through this most beautiful and varied of countrysides without unknowingly trespassing or losing your way. The first to create such a system in a national park, Exmoor is still one of the very few, and the system the most extensive of all. In order that the visitor shall not be perplexed by the very profusion, the Authority has published a series of attractively illustrated booklets with full directions and large-scale maps, available from the Information Centres. And if you have no love for strenuous trekking but find that sometimes, with secure delight, the upland hamlets will invite, the Authority's pamphlets will tell you all you need to know for 'A Walk through Exford', 'through

National Park Information Centre at Combe Martin.

Dulverton,' 'through Lynton' or 'from Simonsbath' and half a dozen places more.

If on the other hand, you take your walking more seriously, Exmoor has the start of the South West Peninsula Coast Path which follows the coastline all the way from Minehead to Combe Martin and on through North Devon to Cornwall, then back to Dorset along the south coast. But you can walk the path in sections, for just a day or even a few hours.

For those who are interested in activities other than walking, Exmoor offers a wide variety from which to choose. Throughout the park there are stables and riding establishments providing unbeatably the best way of seeing Exmoor; for on horseback, even on a pony, you can see over the hedges and take in the beauty while your pony foots

'Snowdrop valley' in January.

it nimbly over the stones or tussocks. Although not all the countryside is open to riders, there are plenty of waymarked bridleways to follow.

While some of Exmoor's roads will take a cyclist from a little above sea level to 1,500 feet in three or four miles, most of them treat you far more leniently. The main roads are busy in summer, but the lanes and byways are completely free of traffic and will lead you into the heart of farming Exmoor.

Most of Exmoor's rivers and streams, together with the reservoirs at Challacombe, Nutscale and Wimbleball offer sport to the freshwater fisherman.

The National Park Authority has a leaflet telling anglers how to obtain licences and tickets.

Those of us who enjoy the privilege – that is the word – of living in Exmoor National Park hope that those who come to explore it will find a pleasure that, like ours, grows day by day as the Moor yields up its secrets. Much of the Exmoor scene delights on the instant – the flame of sunset over Dunkery, the winding red-banked lanes near Withycombe, the tumbling cascades in Worthy Woods, the gold and purple glory of late summer on North Hill, the ponies and the wild red deer. But there remains an inner Exmoor, a spacious yet intimate Exmoor, to be discovered, and for that time and patience hold the keys. And that means, we hope, that you, the patient, quiet, seeking, enquiring visitor, will come again and again.

Daffodils in an orchard on Porlock Hill.

Selected places of interest

ALDERMAN'S BARROW (SS 837432) No aldermen hereabout, but more likely Osmund, who held land in Culbone before 1066. This Bronze Age barrow four miles north of Exford on the boundary of the Forest, is a good landmark and starting point for a walk of seven to eight miles past Larkbarrow and Tom's Hill ruins to the Doone Valley.

ALLERFORD (SS 905470) Delightful hamlet, mainly stone-built, on Horner Water in Selworthy parish, with much-photographed medieval packhorse bridge. Thatched village school now contains local museum well worth a visit (open all year, except Sundays and Christmas Day). Car park and toilets.

ARLINGTON COURT (SS 611405) Stately Regency house, once home of the Chichester family, including Sir Francis the navigator. Gardens and lake, collections of carriages, model ships, pewter and shells. (Open April to October.)

BADGWORTHY WATER (SS 792477) (pronounced Badgery) Beautiful valley leading up from Malmsmead (car park and toilets) to Doone Valley and high moor at Brendon Two Gates. Approach roads from coast steep and narrow and, from Oare, often crowded in summer. For the active, better approached from the moor at Brendon Two Gates.

BARBROOK (SS 715477) Hamlet on West Lyn severely damaged in 1952 flood but bridge rebuilt.

BEULAH CHAPEL (ST 027343) Bible Christian (Methodist) chapel built for iron ore miners on Brendon Hill in 1861 at junction of Taunton – Bampton and Taunton – Wheddon Cross roads. Weekly services still held for mainly farming families.

BLACKMOOR GATE (SS 647432) Main western entrance to national park at crossing of Barnstaple – Lynton and South Molton – Combe Martin roads. Former gateway to the Moor, but an unpromising introduction to the charm of Exmoor. Tidying up is taking place.

BOSSINGTON (SS 898478) Hamlet centred on greensward between Allerford and pebble beach (accessible on foot), mainly owned by National Trust. Footbridge over Horner Water leads to pleasant walks through woods and to Hurlstone (or Orestone) Point. Picturesque village street, interesting cottages characteristic of Porlock Vale – tall chimneys, external bread ovens. Cottage-type Methodist chapel. (Car park and toilets.)

BRATTON (SS 947463) Medieval manor and hamlet one mile west of Minehead on by-road, sheltered from sea winds by North Hill. Claimed as birth-place of judge and jurist Henry de Bracton. (So is Bratton Clovelly, also within the Exmoor area.)

BRENDON (SS 769482) Small village with well-frequented inn, in unusually wide valley of East Lyn, just over (or inside) the Devon border. Name means 'broom hill', no connection with Brendon Hills ('brown hills'). Parish church of St Brendan, Celtic missionary to Devon, nearly two miles from village. Good centre for fishing, walking and riding.

BRENDON TWO GATES (SS 765433) Mainly a cattle grid nowadays at county boundary on Lynton – Simonsbath road where crossed by old Knight Forest wall, but formerly gap closed by ingenious double gate to let riders through and keep stock in. Some parking space. Walks from here westward along boundary to Hoar Oak (landmark) or eastward down Hoccombe Water to Badgworthy and Doone Valley.

BRIDGETOWN (SS 929430) Hamlet in Exton parish on River Exe. Inn and pleasant cricket ground.

BRUSHFORD (SS 920258) Small village near River Barle two miles south of Dulverton. Pixton Park nearby, home of Herbert family. Ancient oak in churchyard, and chapel designed by Lutyens (1926).

BURY (SS 945275) Small, delightful village, some thatch, in Haddeo valley, Brendon foothills, on by-road two miles east of Dulverton. Ford through river and beautiful; very narrow packhorse bridge over. Strongly advised not to attempt either, but very photogenic. Bury Castle nearby, remains of Norman motte and bailey.

CARATACUS STONE (SS 890335) Standing stone near Spire Cross, Winsford Hill; from Dark Ages, inscribed CARATACI NEPVS – 'Grandson or Descendant of Caratacus' – presumably the famous war-chief of the Siluri who defied the Romans.

CARHAMPTON (ST 009425) (pronounced C'rampton) Large, busy village on the A39 three miles east of Minehead, with impressive church and screen. Important enough to give its name to a 'hundred', it once belonged to King Alfred and other kings till 1066, and has legends of King Arthur and the dragons (Viking ships) which ravaged this coast a thousand years ago. The custom of apple wassailing on 17th January (Old Twelfth Night) lingers on here.

CHAINS, THE (SS 735418) Much of Exmoor has lost its old awesome wildness, but this has not. A 'wilderness of waterlogged deer sedge and purple moor grass', it can only be explored on foot or horseback. Best reached from Pinkworthy, Brendon Two Gates via Hoar Oak, or Long Chains Combe. There is little danger of being engulfed nowadays, but you may go in waist deep, and ponies cannot extricate themselves from a 'zog' of that depth.

CHALLACOMBE (SS 694410) Small village on B3224, very narrow here – caution required. The name means 'cold valley', but beautiful situation at foot of hill leading from Devon into Somerset (two miles).

COMBE MARTIN (SS 585465) Pop. 2,279. Long village in deep valley at western extremity of national park. Former quarries and silver mines. Main occupations now tourism and market gardening. National Park Information Centre in Cross Street.

COUNTISBURY (SS 747498) Coastal hamlet at top of famous hill, church and sixteenth century inn, Blue Ball.

COUNTY GATE (SS 794487) Where A39 crosses from Somerset into Devon. Fine views over East Lyn valley. Car park, toilets, National Park Information Centre.

CUTCOMBE (SS 930392) Pop. 304. Main activity centred at Wheddon Cross with combined shop and post office, cattle market and Rest and Be Thankful Inn. Highest point of Dunster – Exeter road (A396), which forms the boundary between Exmoor and Brendon Hills.

DOONE COUNTRY (see BADGWORTHY)

DULVERTON (SS 915280) Pop. 1,288. Quiet little town of narrow streets with medieval bridge over River Barle. Exmoor House, originally workhouse, is now the headquarters of the National Park Authority.

DUNSTER (SS 891416) Pop. 738. Fine buildings from medieval period include castle, church, mill, dovecote, packhorse bridge and Luttrell Arms Hotel (formerly priory). Seventeenth century yarn market. Main car park within walking distance near Dunster Steep, with National Park Information Centre open Easter to October.

EXFORD (SS 855384) (pronounced Ex-*ford*) Pop. 334. In heart of national park. Fishing, hunting and walking centre, hotels, guest houses, youth hostel.

HAWKRIDGE (SS 826308) Lonely village set high on southern border of Somerset overlooking Danes Brook and River Barle. Best reached from Dulverton. Keeps up old tradition of 'revel' in form of summer gymkhana.

HOAR OAK TREE (SS 748430) Ancient boundary mark of Exmoor Forest near former Knight estate wall by Hoaroak Water. Only to be reached on foot. Follow wall westwards from Brendon Two Gates over two miles of hilly country.

HORNER (SS 899454) Cluster of picturesque houses in Luccombe parish by Horner Water. Woodland walk by the water to Cloutsham or Webber's Post. Car park, teas, toilets.

LANDACRE BRIDGE (SS 816362) – pronounced Lann*aker*. Well preserved medieval bridge over River Barle near Withypool Common. Walks up river toward Cow Castle Iron Age fort and Simonsbath.

LUCCOMBE (SS 910445) Picturesque village, mostly owned by National Trust (former estate of Sir Richard Acland). Beautifully set among trees at foot of Robin How. Traces of iron ore mining.

LUXBOROUGH (SS 725495) Village divided into three parts, Kingsbridge, Pooltown and Churchtown, in valley between Brendon and Croydon Hills. Secluded setting, on banks of stream.

LYNMOUTH (SS 725495) Built alongside river and sea, and famous for its picturesque setting. Largely rebuilt after disastrous flood of 1952. National Park Information Centre on Esplanade with features of special interest. Cliff railway connects with Lynton.

LYNTON (SS 720495) Pop. 1,655. Small hilltop town, developed as holiday resort in nineteenth century. Interesting Exmoor Museum at St Vincent's Cottage. Information Centre in Town Hall.

MINEHEAD (SS 970465) Pop. 8,449. Chief holiday resort in West Somerset. Wide shopping street in Parade and Avenue, grievously vandalized by mid-twentieth century developers. Interesting old parts around quay and St Michael's church on North Hill. Hobby horse with dancing attendants parades the district on May Day.

OARE (SS 802473) Pop. 54. Secluded parish, with church the setting for wedding of Jan Ridd and Lorna Doone. Field Centre at Malmsmead open mid-week in summer.

PINKWORTHY POND (SS 724424) (pronounced 'Pinkery'). Pond, seven acres in area constructed at source of River Barle about 1830. Property of National Park Authority; approached by footpath from B3358 between Challacombe and Simonsbath.

PORLOCK (SS 885478) Pop. 1,231. Large busy village encircled by hills except on seaward side. Repays a lengthy visit. Early closing Wednesday.

PORLOCK WEIR (SS 865478) Coastal hamlet and port, now used mainly by pleasure craft. Pebbly beach, old inn, car park, toilets.

SELWORTHY (SS 920468) Pop. 475 (including Allerford). Famous village of thatched cottages around green, built for pensioners by Sir Thomas Dyke Acland in mid-nineteenth century. Once part of Holnicote Estate, now owned by National Trust. Information Centre at the Green. Fine church on hill with extensive views across Porlock Vale to Dunkery.

SIMONSBATH (SS 775394) (pronounced 'Simmonsbath'). Thought to mark the place where Siegmund's *path* crosses the River Barle. Centre of Knight empire in nineteenth century. Two hotels, car park and picnic site.

TARR STEPS (SS 868322) Ancient causeway over River Barle – though of unknown age – finest example of clapper bridge. Turn off B3223 on Winsford Hill, but drive with caution. Road often congested. Car park and toilets nearby, but Steps should be approached on foot.

TIMBERSCOMBE (SS 956420) Pop. 347. Red sandstone village in vale of River Avill south of Dunster. Interesting church and chapel.

WINSFORD (SS 905350) (pronounced 'Wince-*ford*'). Attractive village set in wide valley amid wooded hills; best reached from turning off A396. Birthplace of statesman Ernest Bevin. Thatched Royal Oak Inn.

WITHYPOOL (SS 845356) Pop. 199 (including Hawkridge). Ancient settlement on River Barle. Handsome mid-nineteenth century five-arched stone bridge. Novelist Walter Raymond lived here from 1905 to 1914. Blackmore wrote part of *Lorna Doone* when staying at Royal Oak Inn.

WOOTTON COURTENAY (SS 938434) Pop. 238. Village, largely sandstone, stretching for more than a mile along lower slopes of Wootton Common. Wonderful carved bosses in roof of church.

Glossary

adit – opening or passage into a mine

arrish – stubble field

agistment – grazing for payment

awn – beard of barley

barton – farmyard

bizgy (Som.) *two-bill* (Devon) – mattock with blades set at right angles to each other

clapper – bridge of flat slabs

cob – composition of clay and straw for building

combe, coombe – wooded valley, generally steep-sided; hollow in the hills

court – (enclosed) yard attached to farm

deek – to line or face a bank with stones

drift – horizontal or oblique entry to mine; OR drove road

four-cross way – crossroads

goyal – deep cleft in hillside or moorland worn away by water

harbourer – hunt servant who traces lair of deer

heathland – moorland (heather-covered)

hogg – yearling sheep

knap – hillock, hill-crest

lay (hedge) – repair hedge by half-severing saplings, laying them flat and securing them

linhay, linney – shed open in front

lynchet – terrace or ledge

moot – tree stump

more – underground root

orts – food left over after meal

pentice – lean-to shed projecting from main building

rag, ragstone – rough stone breaking into irregular slabs

shillet – shaley rock

shippon (Devon) – cowshed

slot – footprint of deer

soil – (deer) take refuge in water

tallet – loft in outbuilding

tedd – spread new-mown grass or hay for drying

three-cross way – road junction

tufter – hound that drives deer out of cover

urts – whortleberries, bilberries

vuzz – gorse, furze

Bibliography

Enjoying Exmoor, Exmoor National Park Authority, 1985

The Exmoor Bibliography *

The Exmoor Review, Exmoor Society, annually 1959 – present

Allen, N V *Birds of Exmoor*, 1971,* *Churches and Chapels of Exmoor*, 1974,* *Exmoor Handbook and Gazetteer*, 1979,* *Exmoor Locations* (over 2,000 grid references – invaluable), *Exmoor Place Names* (origins, brief descriptions), *Exmoor's Wildlife*, Guest, 1979, *Waters of Exmoor* *

Binding, H and Bonham Carter, V *Old Dulverton and Around* *

Blackmore, R D *Lorna Doone*, 1869, *Clara Vaughn*, 1864, *The Maid of Sker*, 1872

Burton, SH *Exmoor*, Hale, 1984 (new edition; among the very best books on the moor)

Court, G *West Somerset in Times Past*

Court, LH *The Romance of a Country Circuit* (o/p)

Eardley-Wilmot, H *Ancient Exmoor*, 1983*

Farr, G *Ships and Harbours of Exmoor* *

Giddens, C *Flowers of Exmoor*, Alcombe Books, 1979

Grinsell, L V *The Archaeology of Exmoor*, David & Charles, 1970

Grinsell, LV *Early Man (Exmoor's Archaeology)*, Exmoor National Park Authority

Hesp, P *Secret Exmoor*, Exmoor National Park Authority

Hurley, J *Legends of Exmoor*, 1980*

Jefferies, Richard *Red Deer*, 1884 – frequently reprinted

Lawrence, B *Exmoor Villages*, 1984*

Lloyd, ER *The Wild Red Deer of Exmoor*, 1975*

MacDermot, ET *A History of the Forest of Exmoor* (authoritative), David & Charles, 1973

Miles, R *The Trees and Woods of Exmoor*, 1972*

Orwin, CS (revised Sellick, RJ) *The Reclamation of Exmoor Forest* (authoritative), David & Charles, 1970

Patten, R W *Exmoor Custom and Song*, 1974*

Sellick, RJ *The Old Mineral Line* *

Sellick, RJ, Hamilton, C and Jones, M *The West Somerset Mineral Railway*, David & Charles, 1962

Savage, J *History of the Hundred of Carhampton*, 1828 (interesting contemporary views)

* All published by Exmoor Press, Dulverton

The majority of the above are most readily obtainable from either the Exmoor National Park Authority's headquarters, Exmoor House, Dulverton or from Alcombe Books, Alcombe, near Minehead

Useful addresses

Exmoor National Park Authority,
Exmoor House,
Dulverton,
Somerset TA22 9HL
(Tel. Dulverton 23665)

Countryside Commission,
South West Regional Office,
Bridge House,
Sion Place,
Clifton Down,
Bristol BS8 4AS
(Tel. 0272 739966)

Council for National Parks,
45 Shelton Street,
London WC2H 9HJ
(Tel. 01 240 3603)

Exmoor Natural History Society,
24 Staunton Road,
Alcombe,
Nr Minehead
(Tel. Minehead 3760)

Exmoor Pony Society,
Secretary: David Mansell,
Glen Fern,
Dulverton
(Tel. Anstey Mills 490)

Exmoor Society,
Parish Rooms,
Dulverton TA22 2DP
(Tel. Dulverton 23335)

National Trust Estate Office,
Holnicote,
Nr Minehead
(Tel. Porlock 862452)

Somerset Trust for Nature
Conservation,
Fyne Court,
Broomfield,
Taunton
(Tel. Kingston St Mary 587)

Index

Page numbers in *italics* refer to illustrations.

Acland family 36, 45, 84–5, 100,
　101, 121, 122
Alderman's Barrow 119
Allerford 119, 121
Anstey Common *49*, 91
Ansteys, the 30
Arlington Court 119
Ashway Farm 87, 93
Ashway Side 94
Avill, River 9, 12, *85*, 122
　Vale of *66*

Badgworthy 46, 98, 120
　Water *82*, 119
Bampfylde (Poltimore) Mines
　76
Barbrook 54, 119
Barle, River 12, *13, 14*, 38, 47,
　54, 55, *55*, 91, 102, 120–2
　passim
　Valley 77
Barnstaple 30, 52, 119
Beulah 66, 119
Bevin, Ernest 87, 122
Birch Cleave 99, *100*, 101
Black Barrow 46
Blackmoor Gate 119
Blackmore, R D *see* Lorna
　Doone
Blathwayt Estate 101
Boevey, James 33–6
Bossington (Hill) 9, 101, 119
Bratton 119
Bratton Clovelly 119
Bratton Fleming 37
Bray 33
Bray, River 12
　Valley *27*, 98
Brendon 30, 38, 47, 52, 64, 119
Brendon Common 46, 91
Brendon Hill *10*, 66, 74, *74*, 76,
　77, 119
Brendon Hills 15, 17, 30, 45, 50,
　71, 72, 74, 75, 91, 94, 98,
　101, 119–21 *passim*
Brendon Two Gates 46–7,
　119–21 *passim*
Bridgetown 66, 120
Broad Mead *48*
Brompton Ralph 38, 64
Brushford 120
Burrow Farm *74*
Burton, S H 32, 81, 96, 98
Bury 66, *68*, 120

Caernarvon family 100
Caratacus Stone *27*, 28, 30, 120
Carhampton 29, 81, 120
Cavudus Stone 30
Chains, The 52, 53, 55–6, 120
Challacombe 30, 120, 121
　reservoir 117
Chargot 74
Chetsford Water 12
Chichester family 119
Chidgley Farm *60*
Churchtown 121
Clatworthy 64
Cloutsham (Gate) 103, 121
Codsend Moor 94
Coleridge, S T 9
Combe Martin 73, *116*, 117, 119,
　120
Combe Sydenham 64
Combwich 30
Cornham (Ford) 77
Countisbury (Hill) *15*, 30, 64, 87,
　120
County Gate 120
Court, Lewis H 65
Cow Castle *24*, 121
Croydon Hill 98, 101, 121
Culbone 29, 30, 64, 65, 119
　Wood 98
Cutcombe 30, 38, 64, 86, 120

Danes Brook 12, 121
Defoe, Daniel 73
Doone family/Valley 10, 82–3,
　119, 120
Driver 49
Dulverton *13*, 30, 33, 38, 67, *68*,
　73, 87, 98, 112, *113*, 117,
　120, 120–1, 121
Dunkery (Beacon) 7, 9, 14, *26*,
　91, *91*, 92, 98, 118, 122
Dunster 9, *64*, 65, *71*, 72, 81, 85,
　96, 100, 120–2 *passim*
　Castle 64, *85*, 98, 121
　marshes 9
Duredon 49

East Anstey *see* Anstey
East Lyn *see* Lyn
Emmet's Grange 49
Exe, River *7*, 12, 14, 15, 55, 91,
　102, 120
Exe Head 92

Exford 30, *37*, 38, 39, *40*, 41–3,
　47, 52, 65, 66, 96, 116, 119,
　121
Exmoor Natural History Society
　90
Exmoor Society 56, 57
Exton 120

Farley Water 102
Five Barrows 26, *26*, *80*
floods 53–4
Florence Mine 76
Foreland Point *12*, 103
Forestry Commission 55, 56,
　101
Fortescue Estate 106–7
Froude, Parson Jack 87, 89

Glenthorne 100, 101, 103–4
Grabbist 98, 101
Grinsell, L V 22, 23
Gupworthy 66, 72, 74, 75

Haddeo, River 12
　Valley 98, 120
Haddon Hill 93
Halliday family 100
Hangman 91
harepath 30, *31*, 32–3, 81
Harington 65
Hawkcombe 98, 101
Hawkcombe Head 22
Hawkridge *14*, 121, 122
Heasley Mill 76, *77*
Heddon, River/Valley 12, 100
Heddon's Mouth 82
Herbert family 86, 120
Hinkley Point 9
Hoar Oak 120
Hoar Oak Tree 121
Hoaroak Water 55, 121
Hoccombe Water 120
Holnicote 85, 122
Honeymead 53
Hopcott Common *9*
Horner 121
Horner Valley 100
Horner Water 9, 98, 119, 121
Horner Woods 100
Horsen 49
Hurlstone (Orestone) 119

Ilfracombe 19, 73
Iron Hill 74

Jefferies, Richard 14, 96, 97–8, 105

Kentisbury Down 22
Kingsbridge 121
Kingsbrompton 38, 65, 66
Kingsdown Clump 101
Kinsford Water 12
Knap Down *73*
Knight family 41–2, 45–51, 52, 77, 78, 84, 99, 107, 120–2 *passim*
Knowstone 87

Landacre (Bridge) 54, *54*, 121
Larkbarrow 49, 52, 114, 119
Leigh Barton 81
Leighland *10*
lifeboatmen 87
Long Chains Combe 120
Long Holcombe 59
Longstone *26*
Longstone Allotments 22
Longstone Barrow *26*, 53
Lorna Doone 82–4, 121, 122 *see also* Doone family/Valley
Lower Barle *see* Barle
Luccombe 65, 121
Luckwell Bridge 66
Luttrell family 85, 100, 121
Luxborough 38, 65, *70*, 71, 74, 79, 121
Luxborough Brook 12
Lyn, River *11*, 12, 54, 55, 91, 119
Valley *81*, 120
Lynmouth 11, *15*, 47, 54, *56*, 87, 121
Lynton *15*, 30, 47, 52, 57, 61, 102, 117, 119–21 *passim*

Malmsmead 119, 121
Mannacot Farm *109*
Marsh Farm 77
Martinhoe 28, 33
Minehead 9, 61, 63, 81, 98, 101, 102, 103, 117, 119–21 *passim*
mineral line 74–6, *76*
Mole, River/Valley 12, 98
Mole's Chamber 32, *32*
Molland 65, 72
Molland Common 91, 94
Monksilver 98

National Trust 100, 101, 119, 121, 122
Nettlecombe (Court/Park) 44, *44*, 45, 64, *64*, 65, 86, 98, 100
New Mills *70*, 79
North Hill 9, 91, 100, 101, 104, 118, 119, 121
Nutscale reservoir 117

Oare *29*, 30, 64, 65, 119, 121

Old Burrow 28
Old Cleeve *60*
One Barrow 26
Orestone (Hurlstone) 119

Parracombe (Common) 22, 30
Parrett, River 30
Pinkworthy (Pond) *46*, 47, 49, 52, 92, 120, 121
Pixton 86, 98, 100, 120
Poltimore (Bampfylde) Mines 76
ponies, wild 93–4, *94*, 107–8, 118
Pooltown 121
Porlock 29, 30, 32, 63, 65, 67, 82, 99, 102, 121
Bay 32, 103
Common 91
Hill 87, *118*
Vale of 9, 63, 90, 119, 122
woods 101
Porlock Weir 9, 47, 77, 87, *88*, *102*, 103, 121

Quantocks 32, 96

Raleigh Cross Inn 75
Raymond, Walter 122
Relph, Revd Joseph 41–2
Roadwater 66–7, *67*, 71, 72
Robbins, Tom 86
Robin How 121
Rodhuish 64
Rogers, Ebenezer 74
Russell, 'Jack' 87

Sandhill 82
Sandyway 47
Scob Hill *17*
Selworthy (Green/Woods) 9, *63*, 65, *79*, 83, 85, 98, 100, 119, 121–2
Setta Barrow 26
Sharp, Cecil 82
Shoulsbarrow/Shoulsbury 12, *27*, 28
Simonsbath 30, 41, 42, 47, 48, 49, 52, 54, *62*, 77, 99, *100*, 117, 120–2 *passim*
House 35, *35*, 36, 47
Sinclair, Geoffrey 57
'Snowdrop Valley' *117*
Somerset and North Devon Coast Path 103
Somerset Trust for Nature Conservation 103
South Barton Wood *14*
South Molton 47, 52, 77, 83, 119
South West Peninsula Coast Path 117
Spire Cross 120
Stoke Pevo 64

Swimbridge 87

Tabor Hill 76
Tarr Steps 54, *55*, 122
Taunton 30, 119
Timberscombe 9, 29, 65, 66, *66*, 122
Tiverton 84, 96
Tom's Hill 49, 52, 119
Treborough 65, 71
Trentishoe 65, 82, 91
Trevelyan family 45, 85–6, 100
Twitchen 30
Two Barrows 26

Upton 66

Valley of Rocks *18*, *19*, 91
Vancouver, Charles 41

Warren 49
Warren Farm *59*, 93, 114
Watchet 30, 32, 74, 81
Watersmeet 100
Webber's Post 121
West Lyn *see* Lyn
West Somerset Railway 9
West Somerset Small Industries Group 79
Wheal Eliza mine 77–8, 78
Wheddon Cross 69, 119, 120
Wheeled Stone Cross 30
Whybrow, Charles 23
Williams, Sir George 86–7
Wimbleball reservoir *20*, 93, 117
Winsford 30, 38, 52, 65, 66, 87, 122
Winsford Hill *27*, 28, 30, 91, *91*, 94, 105, 108, 120, 122
Wintershead 49, 50
Withiel Florey 38, 64, *65*
Withycombe 65, 82, 118
Withypool 38, 66, 122
Common 91, 94, 121
Woody Bay 100
Wootton Courtenay 65, 122
Worthy Wood(s) 98, 118

Yeo, River 12
YMCA 86